Quick Quilting

Quick Quilting

- **Rotary Cutting**
- **Machine Piecing** • **Machine Appliqué**
- **Machine Quilting**

Kim H. Ritter

THE QUILT DIGEST PRESS
NTC/Contemporary Publishing Company

Library of Congress Cataloging-in-Publication Data

Ritter, Kim.
    Quick quilting : rotary cutting, machine piecing, appliqué, and
quilting / Kim Ritter.
        p.   cm.
    Includes index.
    ISBN 0-8442-2656-4
    1. Patchwork—Patterns.   2. Machine quilting.   3. Machine
appliqué.   4. Rotary cutting.   I. Title.
TT835.R574   1997
746.46—dc21
                                                        97-15390
                                                              CIP

Edited by Clare Hill
Designed by Sue Rawkins and Tony Cohen
Cover design by Kim Bartko
Photography by Lou Jeffrey
Styling by Kate Hardy
Illustrations by Linda White and Brihton Illustration

First published in the United Kingdom by Merehurst Limited
Ferry House, 51–57 Lacy Road, Putney, London SW15 1PR

This edition first published 1997 by The Quilt Digest Press
An imprint of NTC/Contemporary Publishing Company
4255 West Touhy Avenue, Lincolnwood (Chicago), Illinois 60646-1975 U.S.A.
Copyright © 1996 by Merehurst Limited
Color separation by P&W Graphics Pte Ltd, Singapore
Printed in Italy
International Standard Book Number: 0-8442-2656-4
18   17   16   15   14   13   12   11   10   9   8   7   6   5   4   3   2   1

CONTENTS

Introduction   6

How this Book is Organised   8
Getting Started   10
Patterns, Fabrics and Colours   12
Making and Using Templates   16
Techniques for Accurate Sewing   17
Quick Cutting Techniques   18
Quick Piecing Techniques   20
Quick Appliqué Techniques   25
Assembling the Quilt Top   26
Assembling the Quilt Layers   28
Quick Quilting Techniques   30
Finishing Techniques   33

PROJECTS   37

Iris Sampler Picnic Cloth   38
Country Kitchen Accessories   44
Ohio Star Quilt   48
Delectable Mountains Quilt   52
Bunny Quilt   56
Nine Patch with Hearts Baby Quilt   60
Country Basket Quilt   64
Rail Fence Wall Hanging   68
Seminole Album Cover   72
Sunshine and Shadows Quilt   76
Bargello Jewellery Roll   80
Lone Star Wall Hanging   84
Reindeer Quilt   88
Granny Smith's Log Cabin Quilt   92
Pineapple Cushion   96
Crazy Quilted Table Runner   100
Leaf Cushion   102
Flying Geese Bag   106
String Pieced Star Quilt   110
String Pieced Wall Hanging   114

Templates   118

Quilting Contacts   125

Index   127

QUILTS AND QUILTMAKING

Every family deserves at least one quilt. They are so wrapped up in our ideals and fantasies about family life and heritage that owning a quilt really does make a house a home. Traditionally, quilts have been handed down through families and can last, in use, for over a hundred years – just getting better and better! They were often made for a bridal trousseau but, today, making a quilt for a family member or close friend is a wonderful way to show how much that person means to you. Not only do handmade quilts have a value and dignity all of their own, they are also heaven to sleep under, providing a unique warmth and sense of security.

Until recently, many people were put off making quilts because it was an extremely time-consuming activity. However, by using techniques such as rotary cutting, strip piecing, machine sewing and other tips I will show you, beautiful quilts can be made in just a few hours – or a few days for the more complicated ones. These new techniques have made quilting within the reach of anyone.

It really is so easy to start quilting. Try one of the smaller projects first, especially if you have very little sewing experience. It also helps to become familiar with your sewing machine and, if I may pass on a word of advice from my father, *always* read the instructions *first*. Make sure you understand them and then follow them, you will save yourself many hours of frustration.

Quilting does not need to be restricted to just making bedcovers. Quilts can be made into wall hangings, clothes, bags, curtains, cushions, decorative features for covering furniture – you name it and it can probably be quilted!

Computers, too, have altered and enhanced the world of quiltmaking. They can be used to draft designs, draw up templates, make shapes for appliqué – there is even a quilters' bulletin board on the Internet!

But be forewarned; quilting can be addictive! Soon you'll be hoarding little bits of fabric all over the house, rummaging through second-hand clothing shops and looking at every scrap of fabric you come across with a view to working it into a quilt. Quilting ideas will be swirling through your head, so keep a notebook for the best ideas. Join a quilting guild or class and soon your quilting friends will be multiplying as quickly as the bits of fabric in your scrap bag.

Today, quiltmaking is popular all over the world. It is a common bond that knows no boundaries. It brings people together just as it did during the American frontier days when the quilting bee was a very popular form of socialising.

Quilters are great people. They are quick to praise and quick to share hints and tips for improving skills.

Why not join them?

How This Book is Organised

This book is designed to help you make a quilt with the minimum amount of trouble. It is broken down into various sections which I strongly advise you to read first.

◆ Getting Started

This section helps you select the equipment and materials for making a quilt. It gives advice on the layout of your sewing area and includes help with selecting fabrics and colours.

◆ Techniques Section

The next section is perhaps the most important as it covers the basic steps of making a quilt and explores some of the shortcuts quilters use today to speed up the process. Read this section *before* beginning a project. Each project will give you references to the sections relevant to making the quilt. Refer back to these sections whenever you need to!

◆ Projects

The projects in this book vary in how easy or difficult they are to do – although none are particularly hard. They are given a star rating to denote the level of skill required. These are:

* VERY EASY Suitable for an absolute beginner.

* * MODERATELY EASY This indicates that a beginner could do the quilt provided they had a reasonable degree of sewing experience.

* * * SKILL REQUIRED This does not indicate that the quilts are difficult, just that if you have never quilted before you might find it a bit daunting to take on one of these bigger projects.

◆ Fabric Requirements

The fabric requirements have been calculated using the standard quilting cotton width of 110 cm (44 in), with selvages removed. A generous amount of fabric has been specified for each project to allow for shrinkage of the fabric (always wash, dry and iron the fabric before you start cutting out) and the odd mistake or two! The sizes of the backing and batting given for each project includes extra fabric which is trimmed before binding. As the backing is such a large piece of fabric, it can be pieced if necessary (see page 28).

◆ Templates

Full-size patchwork templates are included at the back of the book for those few projects which require them, but most of the pieces for the projects are cut with a rotary cutter and so no templates are required.

- The solid line of the template is the cutting line.
- The dotted line is the sewing line.
- An arrow indicates the straight of grain of the fabric. Align the arrow with the crossgrain or lengthwise grain.
- A .75 cm (¼ in) seam allowance has been added.

The appliqué templates you require for certain projects have been reduced but you can enlarge them to the correct size, referring to the instructions on the template pages (page 118-123).

The appliqué templates provided indicate only the sewing line. For freezer paper appliqué, cut out the fabric with about .75 cm (¼ in) of extra fabric around the freezer paper template. For fusible web appliqué, cut on the sewing line. The cut edge does not require a turn-under allowance as it is covered with satin stitch.

◆ Threads

Always use cotton mercerised thread in both the bobbin and needle, unless otherwise stated.

◆ Reference Guide

On each of the projects there is a quick reference guide to the techniques you will use. These techniques are explained in full in the techniques section (pages 12-36).

MEASUREMENTS

◆ When cutting, sewing and assembling the quilt you must work in only *one* set of measurements. Choose *either* metric *or* imperial – but don't work in both. If you do, your quilt will not be accurate – in fact, it will look very strange.

At first, some of the conversions may look very odd. For example: The seam allowances in metric are always .75 cm (¼ in) and you may be tempted to round it up to 1 cm. *Don't.* These measurements are based on those given on a quilting ruler and so they are accurate and consistent, whichever set of measurements you choose to work in.

Star rating denotes the level of skill required ———————————————— SKILL LEVEL: ✳ ✳

Photograph of the quilt helps to identify —————————
fabric placement

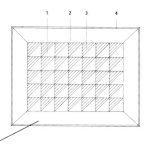

Size of the finished quilt —————————————————

SUNSHINE AND SHADOWS QUILT

◆ Size: 175 x 225 cm (70 x 90 in)

The Amish people of Lancaster County in Pennsylvania have long kept to their traditional values and isolated themselves from outside worldly influences. They scorn the use of modern machinery and still drive around in horse-and-buggies. The Amish quilters are well known for wonderful handsewn quilts in striking colours and this traditional Amish pattern would have been made of solid fabrics throughout, as their religious beliefs led them to think that prints were frivolous.

Nevertheless, you can't get more frivolous than these two prints: one with multi-coloured stars, the other with multi-coloured animals.

The colour scheme is still Amish, with intense colours against a dark background. I have also used the bright solid colours so favoured by the Amish in the pieced portion of the block. The piecing is speeded up by cutting the triangles from a strip pieced unit. This is a quilt that will definitely bring sweet dreams!

Fabric panel gives all the information needed
on·the quantities of fabric and how to cut it,
as well as listing any additional equipment
you may need

FABRIC QUANTITIES AND CUTTING INSTRUCTIONS

1 ◆ MULTI-COLOURED STARS PRINT: 1.75 x 110 cm (1 ⅞ x 44 in)
Cut eighteen squares 27.5 cm (10 ¾ in). Cut across one diagonal to form 36 triangles. (there will be one triangle left over which you won't need).

2 ◆ MULTI-COLOURED ANIMAL PRINT: 2.75 m (3 yds)
Cut two borders 100 x 26.5 cm (80 x 10 ½ in).
Cut two borders 250 x 26.5 m (100 x 10 ½ in).

3 ◆ NINE SOLID-COLOURED FABRICS: 35 cm (⅜ yd) each
Cut five 6.5 cm (1 ⅞ in) strips of each of the nine solid fabrics.

4 ◆ BACKING: 185 x 235 m (74 x 94 in)

◆ **BATTING:** 185 x 235 m (74 x 94 in)

ADDITIONAL MATERIALS
◆ **TEMPLATE PAPER:** 27.5 x 27.5 cm (10 ¾ x 10 ¾ in) of template paper for cutting out solid colour templates.

Fabric key indicates the examples of the
different fabrics and helps, with the
photograph above, to identify fabric
placement

SUNSHINE AND SHADOWS QUILT

Quilt assembly

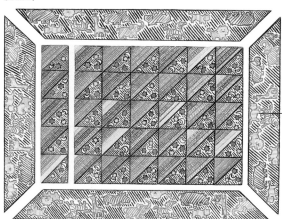

Quilt assembly diagram illustrates how all
the pieces of the quilt top fit together

ASSEMBLY INSTRUCTIONS

1 Sandwich the quilt top with the batting and backing fabric. Pin and baste.

2 To quilt, machine diagonally across the quilt top, using the quilting-in-the-ditch technique at the edges of the strips. Machine stitch the borders using a free motion pattern.

3 Trim the batting even with the quilt top. Self-bind the quilt edges with the backing fabric.

◆ EASY REFERENCE

Making and Using Templates: **page 16**

Mitring borders: **page 27**

Quick Quilting Techniques: **page 30**

Self-binding finish: **page 33**

Easy reference guide shows which
techniques are used in the project and
where to find instructions for them

GETTING STARTED

◆ BASIC PREPARATION

No matter what type of quilt you decide to make, there are a few basic steps which should always be followed:

* **1** Assemble the necessary tools and equipment.
* **2** Choose the pattern, colour scheme and fabrics.
* **3** Prepare sewing area, the fabrics, and the templates.
* **4** Make a test block.
* **5** Cut out all the fabric pieces.
* **6** Piece or appliqué by hand or machine into blocks.
* **7** Press the seam allowances.
* **8** Sew into rows.
* **9** Sew the rows together.
* **10** Add the borders.
* **11** Press the top with a steam iron.
* **12** Prepare the backing fabric and batting.
* **13** Mark the quilting pattern on the top.
* **14** Layer the quilt 'sandwich' – quilt on top, batting in the middle and backing fabric on the bottom. Pin and then baste.
* **15** Use hand-quilting, machine-quilting or tying to secure the layers. Remove basting stitches.
* **16** Bind or finish the edges of the quilt.
* **17** Attach a sleeve if you are going to display the quilt.
* **18** Sign and date your quilt!

TOOLS AND EQUIPMENT

Graph paper: For drafting templates and planning designs.

Permanent fine-line markers: For making templates and for signing your quilt. Never use a ballpoint pen on templates or fabric as the ink will spread, make a nasty mess that is impossible to wash out!

Template plastic: Use a gridded or non-gridded plastic template sheet or stencil acetate to make your templates. Cardboard may be used but it doesn't hold an edge as well as plastic and you cannot see through it to position your fabric.

Craft knife: For cutting out templates.

Computer: The computer can be a great tool for designing quilts and for drafting patterns. I use my computer to print foundation patterns, graph paper and templates. It can also be used to colour and design blocks and quilts. It is even possible to print directly from your computer onto fabric using a standard printer. Iron the fabric on to an A4 size sheet of freezer paper, trimming off all the dangling threads. Care should be taken if doing this, as you may find your printer objects to the fabric going through the machine and makes a nasty jam. If you're going to try this method, use an old printer!

Marking pencil or pen: Use water-soluble pencils and pens for marking the quilt top. Always test your marking tools on the fabrics before making the quilt to ensure that they will wash out.

Masking tape: This can be used to mark the quilting line when quilting .75 cm (¼ in) from the seam.

Set square: A 30 cm (12 in) right-angled triangle is always useful.

Rotary cutter and mat: A large rotary cutter and spare blades will be needed. Choose the model that fits best in your hand. Choose a mat at least 45 x 60 cm (18 x 24 in), or bigger if possible.

Rotary Ruler: A clear plastic quilting ruler is used for measuring and cutting strips, squares, triangles and diamonds. My favourite size is 15 x 60 cm (6 x 24 in) with accurate .25 cm (⅛ th-inch) markings. It should have 30, 45 and 60° angles marked. *Always* use one – and only one – ruler per project to insure consistency of measurements.

Scissors: A good pair of fabric scissors and a pair of paper scissors will be needed.

SEWING NEEDS

Freezer paper: For machine appliqué. This is available from specialist quilting shops. If you have trouble finding it you could try mail-order outlets.

Light typing paper: For making foundations.

Paper-backed fusible web: Used for machine appliqué.

Foundation material: When doing foundation piecing you can use either paper, fabric or tear-away stabiliser as the foundation.

Glue stick: A water soluble glue stick (the type used on paper) for machine appliqué.

Hoop: A small embroidery hoop can be used when doing free motion quilting. A large quilting hoop is suitable if you are hand-quilting without a frame.

Invisible nylon thread: For machine appliqué and for machine quilting.

Iron: A good steam iron is vital for pressing seams. An old iron is useful for applying fusible webbing for machine appliqué. Keep some iron cleaner handy for cleaning off the iron, and use only mineral water in the iron's steam reservoir.

Mercerised cotton thread or polyester covered cotton thread: For piecing by hand or machine.

Pins: Use good dressmaker pins.

Seam ripper: For unpicking seams. Everyone makes mistakes!

Sewing machine: Piecing can be done much faster when you use a sewing machine. Straight stitching is all that is required for ordinary quilting but a zigzag or blindstitch (blind hemstitch) will be needed when doing machine appliqué. Machine quilting is much easier if your machine has a walking foot as this prevents puckering on the bottom layer. Free motion quilting can only be accomplished if the feed dogs of the machine can be dropped or covered with a plate. A darning foot can also be used for free-motion quilting. Remember to regularly clean and oil the machine, as recommended by the manufacturer.

Sewing machine needles: Always use the appropriate needles for the fabrics you are using and change the needles frequently. Embroidery needles should be used whenever metallic or other unusual threads are required.

Steel safety pins: Use size 2 pins for basting, or use one of the new quilt tacking guns.

Tape measure: A 3 m (120 in) tape measure comes in handy for general measuring, particularly for large areas such as borders.

HAND QUILTING

Although all the projects featured in this book are designed to be made using a machine, some readers may prefer to use hand quilting methods. If this is the case, you will also need:

Thread: Cotton quilting thread.

Needles: Quilters use needles called 'betweens' when hand-quilting. Start with a size 9 and progress to the smaller 10s and 12s for a smaller stitch. Hand appliqué and hand piecing are done using 'sharps' needles ranging in size from 8 to 12.

Thimble: Wear a good thimble on the middle finger of your quilting hand. I prefer the type with a raised edge because it does not slip very easily. Some quilters prefer to use a leather thimble so they can feel the needle when it pierces the fabric. Some also wear a thimble on the underneath hand on the middle or first finger.

SETTING UP YOUR SEWING AREA

◆ Make sure you have adequate light for sewing. A comfortable chair which supports your back is also necessary. A secretarial chair is perfect. Next to the sewing machine, set up a small pad or ironing board for pressing your blocks as you go. Place this on the right of your sewing table.

When machine quilting, move the little table to the left of your machine to support the weight of the quilt.

PATTERNS, FABRICS AND COLOURS

The excitement of making a quilt has much to do with creating interesting visual effects by using differently patterned fabrics or assembling contrasting fabrics in various combinations. There are many traditional patterns used in quilting but quilters today have contributed much to the art by creating new designs in much the same way as modern artists break the conventional rules of painting to open up whole new ways of viewing traditional subjects. However, if you are new to quilting it is probably best to start with the tried and tested methods of combining patterns before you go on to creatively break all the rules.

◆

◆ CHOOSING PATTERNS

There are three basic types of quilt tops:

Whole cloth quilts
These feature only the quilted design. The top is one whole piece of fabric.

Appliquéd quilts
These use a base layer with other layers of fabric applied onto the base.

Pieced quilts
These are made up of small patches sewn together, seam to seam. Pieced quilts can be:

One patch designs, in which only one shape is repeated over and over. These include clamshell quilts and hexagon quilts. These are traditionally done with the English paper-piecing method. In this method a paper template is cut out (without seam allowances) for each patch in the quilt. Fabric is then basted over the paper with the seam allowance of the fabric brought to the back side of the paper template and hand basted in place. The patches are then whipstitched together by hand. These were the earliest patchwork patterns and many are still popular today, although there are now easier ways to make them!

Blocks (or squares). This technique flourished in America. The blocks are exactly what they say they are: pieces of fabric of equal size, usually square but sometimes rectangular, which are sewn together. The effect of using blocks is to make a geometric pattern on the finished quilt.

Blocks can also be made up of smaller squares or even triangles, to make a main block. The easiest blocks to use in a quilt have larger and fewer patches to sew together. Bigger patches are also easier to handle and much quicker to assemble. The number of places where many seams match within a block can also affect the difficulty of sewing. Inset seams increase the difficulty of making a block and curved seams are more difficult to sew than straight seams.

FABRIC WIDTHS

◆ The fabric widths for this book are all calculated on the basis that a standard 110 cm (44 in) width fabric has been purchased and that it has then been washed (to allow for shrinkage) and had the two selvage edges removed prior to use. The fabric you will be working with will therefore be slightly smaller than 110 cm (44 in) in width.

Block names
The blocks are named according to the number of divisions within the block.
Nine-patch: *These have nine divisions in the patch.*
Five-patch: *These have twenty-five divisions.*
Four-patch: *These can have four or sixteen divisions.*

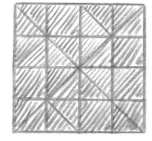

Four Patch Design

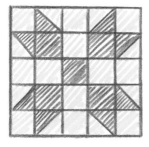

Five Patch Design

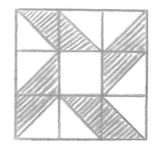

Nine Patch Design

◆ CHOOSING FABRICS

When making the quilts in this book you won't always be able to match the colourways or designs I have used – but it is still important to choose the right fabric. If your quilt is going to be a display item it is possible to combine different types of fabric together, such as velvets, silks, woollen mixes and glazed cottons. However, if it is going to be used, it has to be washable or capable of being dry-cleaned. Mixing different types of fabrics together can be tricky – will some of them shrink? Will others run in the wash? Are some heavier than the others, causing a distortion of the final quilt top? Will conflicting grains of mixed fabrics work together? Not only do these factors have to be considered, we also have to think about how the different fabrics combine in print size and colour to produce different effects. This section deals with these various considerations.

FABRIC GRAINS
Fabric has three grains:
Crossgrain:
This has the grain running the width of the fabric, from selvage to selvage.
Lengthwise grain:
This runs up the length of the fabric.
Bias grain:
This grain runs at a 45° to the straight of grain.

Lengthwise and crossgrain are both on the straight of the grain. In this book pattern templates for piecing and appliqué will show which way to lay the template on the fabric when cutting out. This is shown by an arrow on the template pointing along the straight of the grain. Always place the arrow running parallel with the crossgrain or lengthwise grain of the fabric.

FABRIC PREPARATION
The success of a quilt will depend on how well you have prepared your fabric beforehand. Always remove the tightly woven edges (selvages). If you leave these on and include them in your pieces the seams will pucker and bunch. Pre-wash your cotton and cotton-blend fabrics before using them in a quilting project. Wash each fabric separately in hot water with a scrap of white fabric to remove all finishes, to pre-shrink and to see if any of the fabrics run. If the fabric does run, don't use it. You don't want to spend

Positioning templates

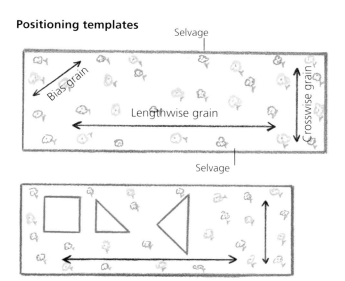

Templates are positioned on the fabric to match the grain.

time on a quilt only to see it pucker and pull out of shape once its been washed! After washing, dry the fabric but leave slightly damp. Straighten the grain of the fabric by tugging on the bias. Iron the fabric while still damp and, if desired, use a spray starch to restore the stiffness of new fabric. This can make it easier to handle the fabric during sewing. If using a spray starch, read the directions on the can and lower your iron temperature to prevent scorching.

FABRIC TYPES
The best fabric for most projects is 100% cotton because it is washable, takes a crease well and does not fray too much. It is possible to use other materials such as silk but only if the item will not need to be washed. Sometimes the only fabric you can find which is the right colour may be in a poly-cotton blend. This will probably be fine, except if you are using it for appliqué shapes as it tends to fray and this may cause problems.

BACKING FABRIC
For the backing fabric I would recommend using 100% cotton. Using an old sheet is fine if you are machine quilting but not if you are hand quilting because the thread count is so high that it makes it difficult to sew.

BATTING
I have used 100% needle-punched cotton batting (also known as wadding) in all of the projects in this book but other types of batting work well. Always read the manufacturer's instructions to see if the batting requires pre-washing or fluffing in the dryer before use.

Rail Fence Quilt
Contrast in value.

Delectable Mountains Quilt
Contrast in print scale.

Lone Star Quilt
Analogous colours.

Iris sampler Quilt
Complementary colours.

◆ CHOOSING A COLOUR SCHEME

Choosing a colour scheme can seem difficult, but it is really one of the most rewarding parts of making a quilt. First, you must determine the purpose of the quilt. Is it for your bedroom or some other part of your house? Will it hang on a wall or stay on the bed? Consider, too, how the quilt will be used and by whom. Is it a gift or is it for you?

Try to capture a mood with your quilt. Do you want a soothing, peaceful quilt or do you want an exciting, daring quilt? Bright bold, fabrics will give excitement while peaceful pastels and cool colours such as blues and greens can be most restful for a bedroom. Be conservative in colour schemes if you want your quilt to be peaceful and comfortable; be a little adventurous if you want your quilt to sing!

◆

CONTRAST IN VALUE

Add more interest by introducing contrast in value. Value describes the relative lightness or darkness of a colour. Most quilts have at least one light, one medium, and one dark fabric. This is a contrast in value.

To detect the value of a fabric to the rest of the chosen fabrics, step back and squint at all the fabrics together. Try to place them from light to dark. Any fabric that is in the wrong position in relation to the other fabrics will stand out when you squint. If you have trouble trying to judge whether a print is light, medium or dark in value, cut out small squares and photocopy the fabrics together. Fabrics of similar value will read as the same shade of grey on a photocopy. Colours of similar value may cause the eye to group the patches into a larger shape. This is why a contrast is necessary.

CONTRAST IN SCALE

Prints come in a range of sizes, referred to as scales. Large-scale prints have large-scale design motifs or elements. Small-scale prints have small motifs.

Create interest and movement in a quilt by using a combination of large-and small-scale prints. Large-scale prints will work best in the larger pattern pieces as, if cut up too small, they loose their effectiveness. Very small-scale prints may look like solids when standing back from a quilt. The use of large-scale prints tends to dissolve the look of boundaries between patches, while solids and small prints tend to read as separate patches. Try to include fabrics with different scales of print.

The colour wheel
The four main colour harmonies are analogous colours, triadic colours, complementary colours and split complementary colours. Their relationship to each other is indicated on the colour wheel.

COLOUR HARMONIES

There are four main colour harmonies – analogous colours, triadic colours, complementary colours and split complementary colours, as explained below. You can stay with these colour schemes or use nature or man-made items as your inspiration. For example, the colours of a flower or those featured in an ethnic print.

Analogous colours
Analogous colours are soothing and comfortable. They are made up of hues that lie close to each other on the colour wheel, for example red-violet, violet, and blue-violet. Two popular analogous colour schemes are based on the idea that colours have temperature. The warm colours, the colours of the sun, lie between yellow and red. Cool colours lie between red-violet and blue-green.

Triadic colours
A triadic colour scheme uses three colours that lie equidistant from each other on the colour wheel. For example, designs that include all three primary colours or all three secondaries are based in a triadic colour harmony. All of these colour harmonies are based on contrasts or differences in colour.

Complementary colours
Complementary colours lie directly opposite each other on the colour wheel. These colour combinations can be made up of reds and greens, blues and oranges, or yellows and purples. These are striking combinations, especially if intense hues are used.

Split complementary colours
Split complementary colour combinations are made up of one colour and the two colours on either side of the complement of that colour. For example, violet combined with yellow-orange and yellow-green. These split complementary colour combinations are very bold and striking, and are made even more so when mixed with fully intense colours.

MAKING AND USING TEMPLATES

Templates allow you to cut out uniform shapes for making patchwork or appliqué shapes. They are made from paper, plastic or metal and you can either buy them or make your own. Traditional English quilts often used paper templates which were made from scrap paper, such as newspaper and old letters. The fabric was folded over the paper and then basted into place. Each paper-covered shape was then sewn together, removing the basting thread but leaving the paper in position. This extremely fiddly technique is seldom used today.

Templates for the projects in this book are given in both metric and imperial measurements. Make sure you stick with one set of measurements and one set of templates per project. The metric templates are identifiable by the suffix 'M' after the template letter and number.

◆

MAKING A TEMPLATE

Trace the templates from the book onto clear quilting template plastic using a permanent fine-line marker. Using this method, you can see through the template to position the pattern on the fabric. In a few projects you will need to draw out your own simple template. To do this, draw the pattern onto squared (graph) paper and then trace it onto the clear quilting template plastic.

Another option is to glue the drafted pattern onto plastic, cardboard or sandpaper (rough side down to grip the fabric during cutting).

Cut out the templates using a craft knife and metal ruler to ensure accuracy. Mark the grainline on the template with an arrow.

PATCHWORK TEMPLATES

Most of the pieced quilts in this book do not require templates but are cut out in batches using a rotary ruler as a measuring device and cutting edge (see *Quick cutting techniques*, page 18). All the seam allowances are included in the instructions, but there is no need to mark the sewing line. The critical line is the cutting line and the patches are aligned along this cut edge, ready for sewing. The patches of fabric are then machine-sewn with the usual seam allowance. Make sure you have made a seam guide which will allow you to accurately sew a .75 cm (¼ in) seam (see *Techniques for accurate sewing*, page 17) when sewing the patches. Templates for the projects included in the book have a solid line showing the cutting line and a dotted line showing the seam line.

The metric cutting measurements given include a .75 cm seam allowance. This is slightly larger than the imperial ¼ in seam allowance equivalent but allows for easy calculations when adding seams to squares, rectangles, diamonds and triangles.

APPLIQUÉ TEMPLATES

The appliqué templates in this book do not include a seam allowance and the edge of the template indicates the sewing line. If you are using freezer paper for your templates, you will need to add a .75 cm seam (¼ in) allowance to turn under the shape before sewing it into position. If you are using fusible web for your appliqué, you do not need to add a seam allowance as the raw edges of the fabric are not turned under but covered in satin stitch. (See *Quick appliqué techniques*, page 25 for more detail on both appliqué methods).

CUTTING FABRIC FROM TEMPLATES

The traditional way to cut fabric patches for hand-sewing is to mark the seam line and cutting line on each patch with a pencil or permanent marker. This is time-consuming and there are quicker methods you can use.

Intricate shapes may need cutting with scissors rather than the rotary cutter. Lay out the fabric on your cutting table with the wrong side facing up. Arrange the templates on the fabric and pin them in place, making sure you align the arrow on the grainline of the fabric. Draw around the template, mark any seam allowances needed and cut out the shapes. To speed things up considerably, you can cut multiple layers of fabric, taking care to pin through all the layers. You can then cut out the shapes required in batches, but remember to go back and mark any seam allowances.

Straight-edged shapes can be cut more quickly using a rotary cutter. To rotary cut multiples of any straight edge shape, layer the fabrics, but do not pin them together. Cut a straight edge on the crossgrain of the fabric using your cutter and quilting ruler. (See *Quick cutting techniques*, page 18). Align one edge of the template along this cut edge. Now cut along the other edges of the templates using the cutter and ruler.

Techniques for Accurate Sewing

The success of any quilt is dependent on the accuracy of the sewing. If the patches do not join up precisely the overall effect of the quilt can be badly affected. Precision is all. Not only must the cutting out of the patches be accurate, but the sewing of the pieces together must also be accurate.

In this book I have largely dispensed with marking seam lines on all of the patches in order to speed up the making of the quilt. However, to ensure that all your seams are 'spot-on' you should first make a seam guide. Once you are confident that your seams are uniform, you should then make a sample block to make sure that your sewing is accurate. If it is not, check your cutting and check your seam guide, as outlined below. This may seem a bit fiddly, but it is vital to the overall accuracy and appearance of the quilt.

◆

Making a Seam Guide

To check the accuracy of your .75 cm (¼ in) seam, cut three strips 4 x 10 cm (1 ½ x 4 in) long. Sew them together along the marked seam line (**fig 1**). Measure the middle strip from finished seam to finished seam. It should measure exactly 2.5 cm (1 in). If not, make a seam guide, as follows:

Place a piece of graph paper under the presser foot of the sewing machine (**fig 2**). Line up the .75 cm (¼ in) line with the needle. Insert the needle in the line. Put a piece of moleskin (available in the foot department of a pharmacy) along the edge of the paper before the dog feeds (**fig 3**). Remove the paper. Use the moleskin as an edge to place the fabric against as you feed it into the machine. You can use layers of masking tape built up to make an edge if moleskin is not available.

Do the accuracy test again with three more strips of fabric and adjust if necessary.

Making a Sample Block

After cutting out and labelling all your templates, cut out some fabric shapes from them to make a sample block. This allows you to detect any problems of accuracy before you begin to cut and assemble the quilt top – potentially saving you a lot of valuable time. This will also give you a chance to see if your fabric choices are working.

Use your ruler to measure the finished size of each patch. If this measurement does not match the finished sizes indicated in your pattern, you may need to remake your template or adjust your seam guide.

fig 2

fig 3

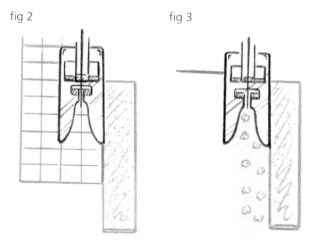

fig 1

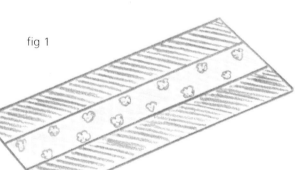

QUICK CUTTING TECHNIQUES

Quiltmakers today use various different techniques to speed up the cutting and assembling of patches and other shapes. Nothing has speeded this process up more, however, than the advent of the rotary cutter. This has revolutionised quilt making. Using this technique you can cut long strips that are then cut into squares, rectangles, triangles or diamonds. Almost any shape can be cut with a rotary cutter.

To rotary cut fabric you need a rotary cutter, an accurate rotary cutting ruler with markings every .25 cm (⅛ in), a cutting mat, and a set square to check angle accuracy.

Set up your mat on a table, holding down the ruler with the left hand and using the cutter in the other hand. Reverse this if you're left-handed. The length of fabric should be extended out to the left.

◆

CUTTING LONG STRIPS

1 Fold the fabric in half on the crossgrain, matching up the selvages. Press the fold. Lay the fabric on the cutting mat with the folded edge nearest to you **(fig 1)**.

2 Line up the set square with the folded edge of the fabric, close to the left edge. Line up the ruler against the edge of the set square **(fig 2)**.

3 Remove the set square and, holding the ruler down firmly in the left hand, make a cut with the rotary cutter, all along the edge of the ruler **(fig 3)**. The ruler must not shift while you are cutting. If it does your strips will not be accurate. You will now have one straight square edge to the fabric.

4 Fold the fabric in half again, making four layers. Working from the straight edge, use the markings on the ruler to measure and cut your strips of fabric **(fig 4)**. Cut against the ruler as before to cut accurately.

5 You will now have one long strip, which can be further cut into shapes. As you cut, stop occasionally and check to see that the strips are still straight by using the set square again.

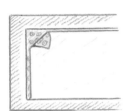

fig 1

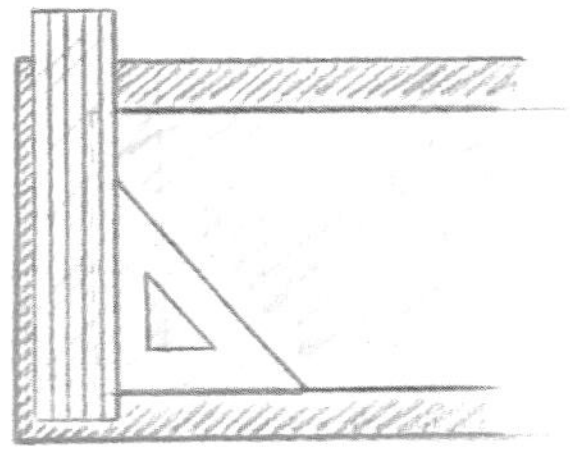

fig 2

fig 3

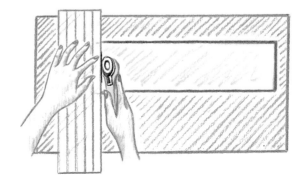

fig 4

CUTTING STRIPS INTO SQUARES AND RECTANGLES

Squares or rectangles are often used in quilt blocks and they can be easily cut, several at a time, without templates using a rotary cutter. Cut the strips to the finished width, plus 1.5 cm (½ in). Turn the strips sideways and cut across them to the finished length, plus 1.5 cm (½ in) (**fig 1**). An allowance of .75 cm (¼ in) for each seam – a total of 1.5 cm (½ in) – has been included in the calculation for the projects so you don't need to add this again (**fig 2**).

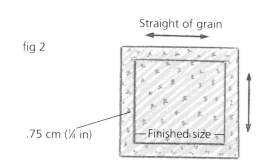

fig 2

Straight of grain

.75 cm (¼ in)

Finished size

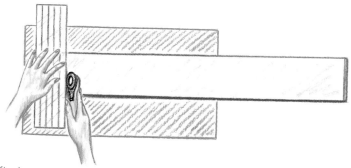

fig 1

CUTTING HALF SQUARE TRIANGLES

Two identical triangles can be cut from a square. These half square triangles will have the straight of grain running along the short sides.

To make half square triangles you simply cut a square into half on the diagonal. Normally, to determine the size of the square to cut for the triangles, you have to allow not only the usual .75 cm (¼ in) seam allowances but also extra fabric for the points. To do this you would add a total of 2.5 cm (⅞ in) to the base of the finished triangle. To make life easier, this calculation has already been done for you in the projects.

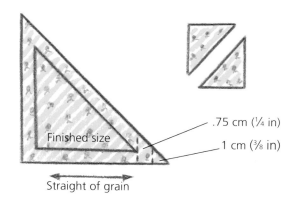

Finished size

.75 cm (¼ in)

1 cm (⅜ in)

Straight of grain

CUTTING QUARTER SQUARE TRIANGLES

When four identical triangles are cut from a square, they are called quarter square triangles. The straight of grain runs along the long edge of the triangle. To make quarter square triangles start by cutting out the squares. Normally, to determine the size of the square to cut for the triangles you allow not only the usual .75 cm (¼ in) seam allowances, but also extra fabric for the points. To do this you would add a total of 3.5 cm (1 ¼ in) to the base of the finished triangle. This calculation has already been done for your in the projects. Cut the square across both diagonals to create four triangles.

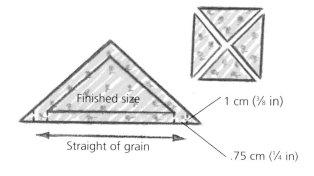

Finished size

1 cm (⅜ in)

Straight of grain

.75 cm (¼ in)

QUICK PIECING TECHNIQUES

Traditionally, patchwork was a method of hand-sewing individual scrapes of fabric together to make a patch and then sewing the patches into bigger units which were then all sewn together to make a finished design. Sometimes units were joined to units which were then joined to further units to produce a complex finished pattern. Today, hand sewing is extremely time-consuming but the same complex patterns can be made – only much, much quicker – using a sewing machine.

◆

MACHINE PATCHWORK

For machine-sewing, the template includes seam allowances but the sewing line is not marked. Cut out the patches in batches of four. The critical line is the cutting line. The patches are aligned along the cut edge. Accurate cutting is essential.

Make sure you have made a seam guide which will allow you to accurately sew a .75 cm (¼ in) seam (see *Techniques for accurate sewing*, page 17). Thread your machine with cotton thread in the bobbin and the top. When machine sewing, place the right sides together, align the edges and pin. Sew through the seam allowances all the way to the cut edge, except when you are sewing a set-in patch. Do not backstitch.

ASSEMBLY LINE PIECING

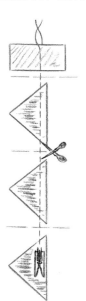

You can speed up the process by pinning all the sets of one type and feeding them into the machine one after another **(fig 1)**. After feeding in the sets, cut the threads between the patches.

STRIP PIECING

Strip piecing is a great time saver. Fabric strips are sewn together along the long edges and then cut across the strips. These pieced strips can then be resewn in a new arrangement. Nine patch designs, chequerboards, chevrons, and diamonds are all possible and easy to do with strip piecing.

fig 1

Strip pieced chequerboards

1 Cut the strips to the widths of the squares needed. An extra 1.5 cm (½ in) for all the seams has been included in the calculations for the projects. Sew the strips together in the desired combinations. Usually you will be working with at least two different sets of strips in different colour combinations **(figs 1 and 2)**.

2 Press the seam allowances towards the darker fabrics. Because chequerboards are usually assembled in alternate light and dark patterns, this allows the seams to fall in different directions. When assembled, the seams will butt up against each other and the seams will match up more easily.

3 After pressing, lay out the joined strip on your cutting mat. Trim off the edge of the strip, being careful to establish a 90° angle before beginning to cut across the strips. Cut the sewn strips into units, using the same measurement as your first strip widths. These units are your pre-sewn rows **(fig 3)**.

4 Sew the rows to the rows cut from the other strip combination(s), in the correct order **(fig 4)**.

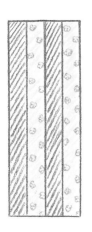

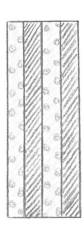

fig 1   fig 2   fig 3

fig 4

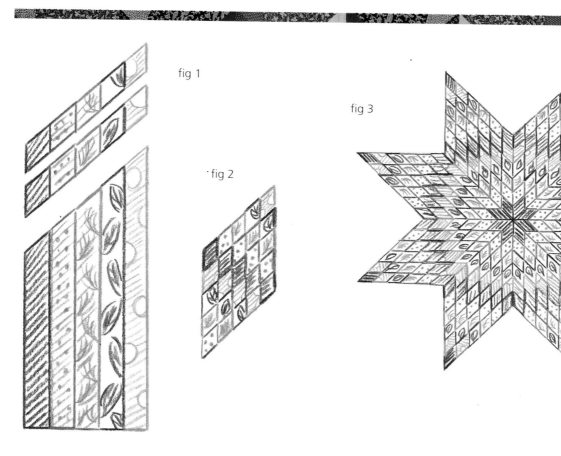

fig 1

fig 2

fig 3

Strip pieced diamonds

To make diamonds, strips of different fabrics are cut and sewn together and then cut on a 45° angle, a 30° angle or a 60° angle **(fig 1).** These units will form rows on a slant, creating a diamond shape when assembled **(fig 2).** The width of the strip needed will be the width of the diamond plus 1.5 cm (½ in) for all the seams. The sewn strips are cut using the same measurement. To make it easier, all these measurements in the projects have been calculated for you. The diamonds made from the sewn strips can be formed into stars **(fig 3)** or other patterns made from diamonds, such as chevrons.

Strip pieced chevrons

Strips can also be assembled so that they form a chevron pattern. To do this, cut one assembled strip of diamonds, **(fig 4).** Cut the second assembled strip on the same angle but as a mirror image of the first **(fig 5).** When assembled, a chevron will appear **(fig 6).** Trim the points to .75 cm (¼ in).

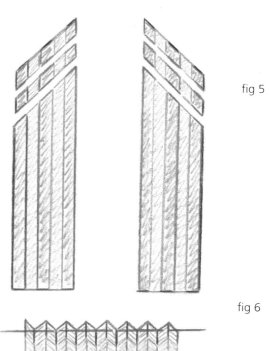

fig 4

fig 5

fig 6

FAST GRID TRIANGLES

Before, when a few half square triangles have been needed, we have cut them from squares (see *Quick cutting techniques*, page 18). However, when many more triangles are required, there is a much quicker way of cutting and piecing them. This can be done by using the grid method, shown below. I use my computer to print my half square triangle grids. I draw them using a drawing programme which has a ruler for accurate templates. Grids printed on rolls of paper are available, as are plastic grids with slots to mark the grids. Be sure to check the accuracy of the seam allowances and the compatibility of the grids with the ruler you will use to measure other patches.

Photocopying the grids can cause distortions in the grid, so always check for accuracy before using them. It is unwise to photocopy a photocopy as any distortion will be magnified.

1 To make fast triangles, cut two rectangles of different fabric. Layer the two fabrics with the right sides of the fabrics together. Place the lightest coloured fabric on top. Press the two layers together with a steam iron. This helps hold them in place while sewing. On the wrong side of the top fabric, use a sharp pencil to mark a grid of squares. The size of the squares is determined by the half square triangle formula: the size of the square is equal to the finished size of the short side of the triangle plus 2.5 cm (⅞ in). All these measurements have been calculated for you in the projects.

2 Draw diagonally through the squares **(fig 1)**. On each side of the diagonal, draw a dotted line .75 cm (¼ in) from the diagonal line. This is the sewing line. Now sew along the dotted lines, skipping over the intersections without sewing, and sew to the end of a diagonal line. Pivot at the end of each line.

3 Cut along all the grid lines to form the half square triangles. You now have lots of pairs of triangles joined to form squares. Press the seams towards the darker fabric.

Note:
You can also draw the grid on graph paper and glue stick it to the top fabric to keep the paper from shifting. Shorten your stitch length to perforate the paper as you sew. Remove the papers after cutting the units apart.

fig 1

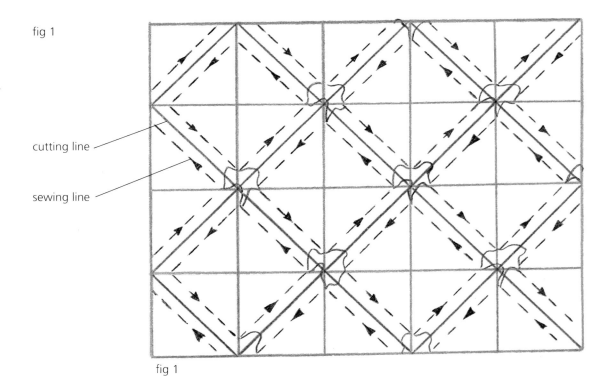

cutting line

sewing line

fig 1

FOUNDATION PIECING

Foundation piecing is a versatile technique. Historically, foundations have been used in many forms. Victorian crazy quilts were often made in this way and log cabin and other strip pieced designs can also be sewn using this technique.

The patches or strips are sewn together onto the foundation of paper or fabric and the seam is pressed open. More strips are sewn in place and pressed open until the block is complete.

Contemporary quiltmakers have extended the foundation piecing technique with a new form in which the foundation is actually sewn from the back. This technique is very accurate and the piecing of intricate designs, such as the pineapple pattern in this book, and piecing miniature quilts with small patches, can be made much simpler.

When combined with blindstitch piecing, curved designs are possible. Because the foundation is stable, fabrics of different weights and types can be used and grainline placement is not very important.

The choice of which foundation to use – paper, fabric or tear-away stabiliser – depends on the type of project, the manner in which you will quilt the item and personal choice. Paper is usually my first choice. It is stable and doesn't distort like fabric will – plus it's cheap and easily available. Thin, almost transparent, paper is best for the method in which the foundation is flipped over and sewn from the back. Paper foundations are torn away after sewing and so no bulk is added to the final project. If you plan to leave the foundation in the quilt, use a light coloured, all-cotton fabric.

Crazy patchwork

Crazy quilting reached its heyday during the Victorian era. These patchworks were usually designed to be displayed rather than used. Many lavish fabric scraps of silk and velvet in different shapes and sizes were used to make items such as tablecloths or parlour throws.

1 Cut a foundation of fabric the size and shape of the finished block, plus a .75 cm (¼ in) seam allowance all round. Cut a five-sided scrap of fabric and place roughly in the centre of the block, right side facing up. Place a second scrap, right side facing down, over the first patch. Sew along one edge of the second scrap, approximately .75 cm (¼ in) from the edge **(fig 1)**. Trim the seam. Open the seam and press in place **(fig 2)**.

2 Next, rotate the foundation and position a third patch over the first two patches. Continue sewing, trimming and pressing until the block is complete **(fig 3)**.

3 Once completed, trim the edges of the fabric blocks even with the foundation **(fig 4)**.

STRING PIECING

String piecing, that is, strip piecing with uneven strips or strings of fabric, is a form of foundation piecing. It is very similar to crazy patchwork but the first pattern is laid down at one end, not in the middle of the foundation.

Crazy patchwork

  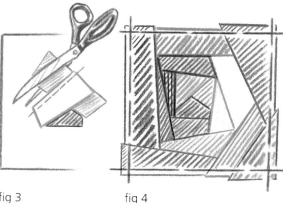

fig 1   fig 2   fig 3   fig 4

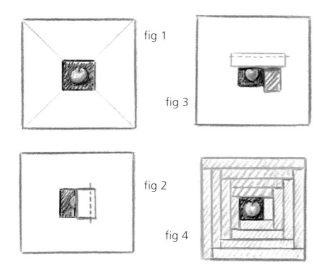

fig 1

fig 3

fig 2

fig 4

LOG CABIN PATCHWORK

Log cabin patchwork is one of the most popular of the traditional quilting patterns and its geometric shapes can be used to form attractive, 3-dimensional visual effects. One of the earliest uses of long strips of fabric was in making log cabin and pineapple designs, where long strips were cut and sewn around a central square. Contemporary renditions of this technique include strip piecing around diamonds, triangles or octagons.

1 To make a log cabin patchwork, cut out the centre square and logs for the cabin according to the pattern directions. Cut a foundation the size of the finished block, plus a .75 cm (¼ in) seam allowance all round. Fold along both diagonals and press. These lines will help you position your centre square and your strips. Place the square in the centre of the block, right side facing up. Align with the diagonal lines on the foundation as a guide **(fig 1 above)**.

2 Place the first of the 'log' pieces, right side facing down, over the first patch. Align the edges carefully. Sew along one edge of the strip .75 cm (¼ in) from the edge **(fig 2)**.

3 Open the seam and press in place. Rotate the foundation by 90° and position another 'log' over the first two patches **(fig 3)**. Add the third and fourth 'logs' to complete the first round.

4 Keep adding strips on each round by gradually increasing the length of the strips **(fig 4)**. Continue sewing and pressing until the block is complete.

TURN-AND-SEW PATCHWORK

For turn-and-sew patchwork, cut strips of fabric according to the pattern requirements. Trace or draw the pattern accurately on light typing paper. (If you use heavier paper a light-box will make it easier to position the patches). Sometimes a few patches are sewn together first before being sewn to the foundation.

1 Attach the pattern to the back of the foundation or use the paper as a foundation. Turn over to the unprinted side and position the first patch, right side up on the unprinted side of the foundation **(fig 1)**.

2 Place a second strip, right side facing down, over the first patch **(fig 2)**. Pin in place.

3 Turn over the foundation to the printed side and sew on the line between patch one and patch two **(fig 3)**. Turn the foundation back to the unprinted side, open the seam and press in place. **(fig 4)**.

4 Trim the seam. Position the third strip **(fig 5)** and continue to turn and sew until the block is complete. Remove the paper.

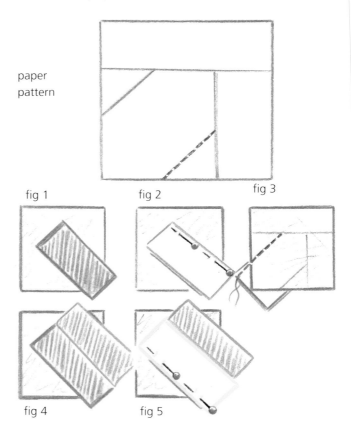

paper pattern

fig 1

fig 2

fig 3

fig 4

fig 5

QUICK APPLIQUÉ TECHNIQUES

Nothing livens up a quilt quite like appliqué shapes. If you want to sew the shapes on by hand, prepare the shapes as for freezer paper appliqué (*see below*) then pin or baste the first shape onto the quilt top. Using a thread colour which matches the shape, begin blindstitching into place using a No.10 sharp needle.

Remember: appliqué templates are printed without seam allowances.

◆

MACHINE APPLIQUÉ

Using your sewing machine to sew the appliqué shapes onto the quilt top really speeds things up. There are two ways to machine appliqué: the bonded method using fusible web and a satin stitch or zigzag stitch, and the freezer paper method using a straight stitch or blindstitch. If you have never done either of these methods before, practice on some scraps of fabric first.

Bonded Machine Appliqué

For the bonded method, fuse paper-backed webbing to the wrong side of the fabric shape, as follows:

1 Draw the shape on the paper backing of the fusible web and then cut it out. Do not add seam allowances. Fuse the shape to the appliqué fabric and cut out. Remove the paper backing and fuse to the background fabric in the appropriate place, following the manufacturer's instructions.

2 Choose a contrasting thread or a thread of the same colour but darker than the appliqué patch. Set your machine to zigzag stitch and lower the stitch length until it sews a satin stitch **(fig 1)**. Stitch all around the shape, through the shape and the quilt top. Pivot with the needle down when you come to corners and points.

Freezer Paper Appliqué

To make freezer paper appliqué shapes, prepare them as follows:

1 Draw the shapes on the uncoated side of the freezer paper and cut out. Place the shape, shiny coated side down, on the wrong side of the fabric and iron into place. Cut out around each shape, adding approximately .75 cm (¼ in) for the seam allowance **(fig 2)**. Some shapes may need to be trimmed slightly closer than this to allow for smooth turning.

2 Use a glue stick to stick the seam allowance to the back of the shape. Pinch around the curves and clip into tight angles to make a smooth curve. Fold at the corners.

3 Position the shape onto the background, using either a straight stitch or a blindstitch by hand or machine.

4 **For straight stitch**, use a thread to match the shape. Sew along the outer edge. Use the top thread to pull the bottom thread to the top at the beginning and end. Tuck in the tails and trim.

  For blindstitch set the stitch length to very small. The 'V' stitch will become almost closed. Position the needle so that the 'V' stitch barely catches the appliqué shape. The straight stitches fall along the edge of the shape on the background fabric **(fig 3)**.

5 Remove the extra layers of fabric by turning the block over and trimming away the bottom layers to .75 cm (¼ in) from the sewing line. The backing fabric will cover up the holes. Dampen the freezer paper and gently tug to remove.

Satin stitch

fig 1

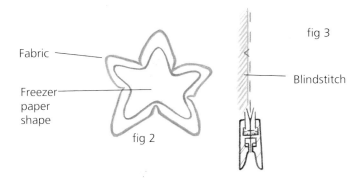

Fabric

Freezer paper shape

fig 2

fig 3

Blindstitch

Assembling the Quilt Top

Making quilts is all about joining up fabric to fabric, blocks to blocks, rows to rows and ending up with a delightfully patterned quilt top. But, to make the most of your top, you must take care to do each of these stages accurately. The finished quilt top should have all its different elements in perfect alignment – and this can be achieved by a few tricks of the trade, outlined below.

◆

Matching up Seams and Points
Matching up the points where seams meet is the secret to accurate sewing. Pressed seams will lay flat and be easier to match up. Whenever possible, press seams toward the darker patch. This will prevent a dark shadow behind the lighter fabric at the seams. Also, press the seams that will match up when sewing in opposite directions. Butt the opposing seams together **(fig 1)**. Use a perpendicular pin where seams meet to position the patches. Use a pin on either side of the upright pin to hold the patches firmly in place. Pin the patches together with the points of the pins pointing to the seam line **(fig 2)**. Sew through the 'X' created by previous seam lines **(fig 3)**.

Sew with even pressure on the foot pedal to make an accurate seam allowance. It is best to sew slowly. Do not pull or tug on the patches as they are being sewn as this will distort the patch. Remember that seams along the bias tend to stretch, so be especially gentle when handling and sewing these seams. Continue sewing, pressing and positioning each patch until your block is complete. A block-piecing diagram for each pattern will help you to decide the order in which you will sew the patches together. When the block is finished, press all the seams and square up the edges using the iron to press the block. Try not to distort the block.

After completing one block it is prudent to measure it to determine if you have pieced and sewn it accurately. Once you are confident that your templates and sewing are accurate, cut and assemble the other blocks.

Set-in Patches
When two patches form an awkward angle, the next patch must be 'set-in' with care **(fig 1)**. Pin the next patch in position aligning one edge with the corresponding edge of one of its neighbours, right sides facing **(fig 2)**. Sew along this seam leaving the needle in the fabric at the corner point. Raise the machine foot and pin the second seam. Lower the foot again, pivot the work on the needle and sew the second seam **(fig 3)**.

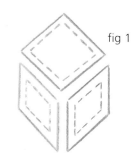

fig 1

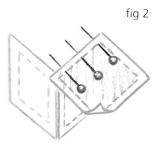

fig 2

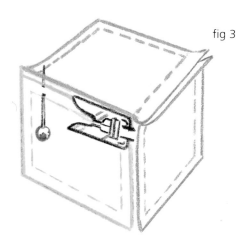

fig 3

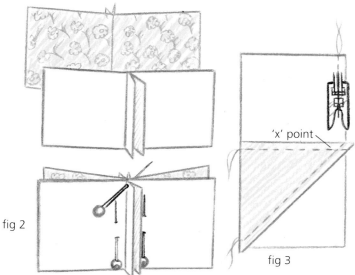

fig 2

'x' point

fig 3

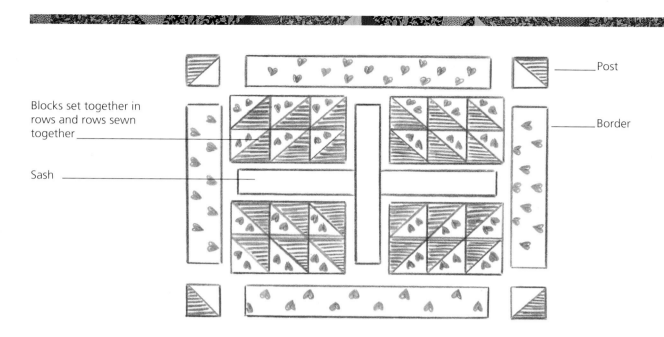

Post

Blocks set together in rows and rows sewn together

Border

Sash

SETTING BLOCKS TOGETHER IN ROWS
Sew the completed blocks together to form rows. Match each point, butt opposing seams together, and pin. Sew a .75 cm (¼ in) seam allowance. Remove pins and check each point for a match. Where seams do not match, unpick about 3-5 cm (1-2 in) around the seam. Realign the points and ease the fabric out between the patches. Resew the seam. Sometimes the blocks are set on point. Here diagonal rows are assembled and triangles are used to finish each row into a square.

ADDING SASHES
Sashes are long strips of fabric which separate or frame a block or a group of blocks. The inside vertical sashes are added as the row is assembled. Horizontal sashes are added at the bottom of each row, before sewing the rows together. Top and bottom sashes are added last.

SEWING ROWS TOGETHER
Press the seam allowances of the rows in alternate directions. Butt the seams against each other. Use a perpendicular pin to match the seam intersections between blocks and wherever seams must match up. Sew the seam and remove pins. If your seams do not match up, unpick the seam around the unmatched point. Reposition and pin. Ease any fullness and sew.

ADDING POSTS
Posts are small squares used on the ends of the borders. They are also used to connect the sashes. The posts add a decorative feature and help frame or emphasise the overall design. Usually they are plain squares of fabric but sometimes they might incorporate a design feature, such as a star or half square triangle. The posts should be added to the ends of the sashes or the border before these elements are assembled.

ADDING BORDERS
Next you will add your borders. These help frame the quilt pattern. The borders should be cut on the length-wise grain if possible. The vertical borders are added first. Position the fabric face down, across the width of the quilt, matching up the centre points. Pin into place, easing in any fullness, and sew with a .75 cm (¼ in) seam allowance. Open out and press. The horizontal borders are positioned in the same way.

MITRED BORDERS
For mitred borders you need to cut a length for each border, adding an extra 25 cm (10 in). Match the centre points of the top border and the top edge of the quilt, laying the border face down on top of the quilt. Mark a point .75 cm (¼ in) from the edge of the quilt and one match point. Match these points and midpoints. Start and stop .75 cm (¼ in) from the edge. Sew the border onto the quilt, starting and ending .75 cm (¼ in) from each corner. Sew on the other border strips. Press and then fold back each corner at a 45° angle, pressing a crease. Place two borders to be mitred right sides together, matching up the crease lines. Sew, beginning .75 cm (¼ in) from the inside corner. Repeat on the other corners and then trim the seams and press open.

ASSEMBLING THE QUILT LAYERS

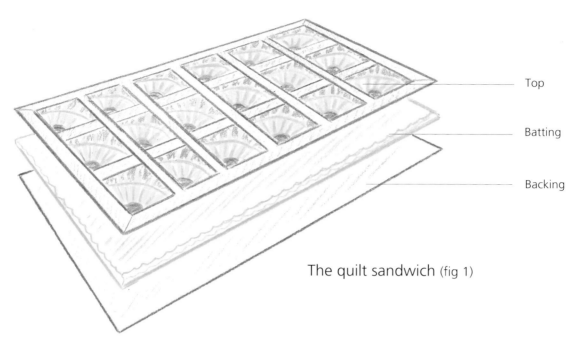

The quilt sandwich (fig 1)

A finished quilt is made up of three layers of fabric sandwiched together: the top layer, the middle layer of batting and the bottom backing fabric **(fig 1)**. The whole of the sandwich can be finished off with either a self-bound binding, an attached binding or continuous prairie points (see *Finishing techniques*, page 33).

◆

PREPARING A BACKING

You will need to have a backing for your quilt which is about 10 cm (4 in) longer and about 10 cm (4 in) wider than the quilt top. The process of quilting will draw up some of the backing and the batting, causing them to get slightly smaller. If the batting and backing are 10 cm (4 in) bigger all the way around the quilt, you will have enough margin for safety. If the quilt is wider than 100 cm (40 in) you will have to join the fabric up. This is usually done by joining the fabric in strips, as shown in **fig 2**. Many quilters today, from necessity or out of creative inspiration, construct a backing from fabric or blocks left over from the project. These backings can be 'crazy quilt' style with random pieces, or can be more formal arrangements of squares, rectangles, strips or other shapes. Some can look just as good from the back as they do from the front!

Joining up fabric to make a backing (fig 2)

seam

seam

Quilt length plus 10 cm (4 in)

Quilt width plus 10 cm (4 in)

PREPARING THE BATTING

To prepare the batting of your quilt, always read the instructions. Some batting requires washing or a breathing period before use, while others require 'fluffing up' on the 'no heat' cycle in the dryer. Follow the instructions that come with the batting.

LAYERING THE QUILT SANDWICH

Press the quilt top and backing and mark your quilting design before layering. Mark the centre of all four edges of the top, the batting and the backing. This will make it easier to centre the quilt layers on top of each other. Mark the centre points of the edges of your work surface with masking tape. Place the backing wrong side up and centred on your surface. Use masking tape or clamps to stretch the backing taut and hold it taut against the work surface. If you don't have a frame, use a large, flat surface to lay the sandwich on, such as a table or floor. To make sure the surface of the table or floor will not be scratched by the needle or pins you will be poking through the layers, you can place your cutting mat under the area you are basting.

Lay the batting out on top of the backing and centre it. Smooth out any wrinkles or bumps. If you are using a fragile batting such as a thin 100% cotton batting, be very careful when handling the batting. If you have bought batting by the yard you will need to butt the batting edges together and then sew them together with cotton thread and a large cross stitch.

Place the quilt top on top of the batting, face up. Smooth out any wrinkles. Make sure that all three edges are centred on top of each other and that you have a generous excess of batting and backing fabric extending beyond the quilt top. You need at least 5 cm (2 in) excess material around all the edges.

BASTING THE LAYERS

After assembling the quilt layers, you are ready to baste. This is done to temporarily hold the layers in place while you quilt. Traditionally, quilts were basted on a full-size home-made quilting frame. The basting was done with cotton thread and a long needle like a darning needle. If you have a frame for basting you will save a lot of time. Follow the instructions for the frame you are using. If you don't have a frame, hold the layers secure by taping all round the edges of the backing and batting **(fig 1)**. For machine quilting, use No. 2 steel safety pins. You will need about 200 for a full-size quilt **(fig 2)**. Begin pinning in the centre and work outward, placing pins about 10 cm (4 in) apart. Try to place the pins in the areas where you will not be quilting. Pin the last rows approximately 2.5 cm (1 in) from the edge. Roll the excess backing and batting to the front and pin around the edge of the quilt. This will keep your batting from shredding around the edge when you finish quilting.

Basting the layers

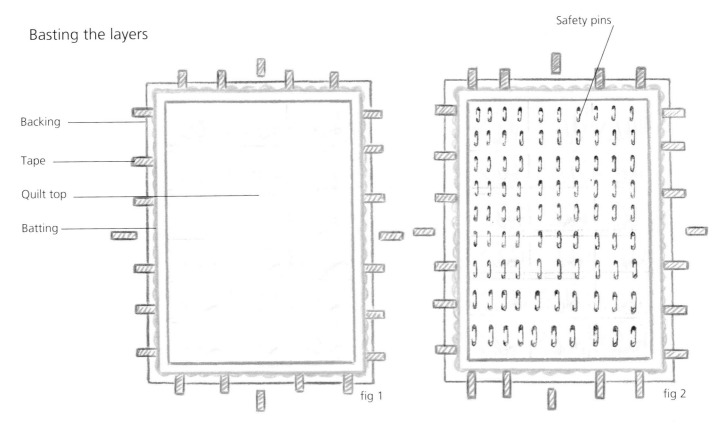

Backing

Tape

Quilt top

Batting

Safety pins

fig 1

fig 2

QUICK QUILTING TECHNIQUES

A large part of the joy of making quilts is watching them come alive with the quilting stitches. By stitching different quilting patterns you can achieve different textual finishes which seems to make the quilt take on an added dimension – some areas are highlighted while others are thrown into relief. When stitching, aim for regular, even stitches so that the effect is uniform.

But first, you must decide which pattern you want. For the quilts featured in this book I have made suggestions or described how I decorated my quilts but you can decide your own. Sometimes the quilting is done without any need for marking the quilt top. You just whizz the quilt through the machine to form whatever pattern you have in mind. However, some of the more complex or regular patterns may need a design line for you to follow. This is done by marking the pattern on to the quilt top before you start sewing.

◆

MARKING THE QUILT TOP

After completing the top and pressing it thoroughly, look over your work for errors and correct any mistakes. You can now choose and mark a quilting design.

Marking the quilting pattern can be done in several ways. For simple outline quilting lines and straight quilting lines you don't need to mark the top but can use .75 cm (¼ in) wide piece of masking tape as a guide (see page 31). For elaborate feather and cables it's best to use a washable lead pencil so that there are no lines left on the fabric, or use a water-soluble pencil or marker pen made for this purpose. Always test the pencil or pen on spare scraps of the fabrics before using! Position the templates carefully. Mark your design on the quilt top as lightly as possible. Don't iron over the marks as heat can set inks and make them permanent.

When doing freestyle quilting designs on the top you do not need to mark out the design, just simply judge the placement by eye when you sew.

Continuous line quilting designs for machine quilting can be marked on the fabric or they can be drawn onto paper and then pinned onto the basted quilt top. After you have finished quilting the design, you just tear the paper away. A little dab of glue from a glue stick (the water soluble kind) will help to hold down paper templates temporarily.

HOW TO MACHINE QUILT

For machine quilting, baste your quilt with safety pins because if you baste with thread it can get caught up in your machine-stitching.

You will need to roll up the part of the quilt which will fit under the machine. Secure the roll with clips made for the purpose or use more safety pins. Fold the excess fabric in your lap to feed through the machine. Use a large table to support the weight of the quilt on the left side of the machine and as it exits from the machine at the back. Quilt the longest lines in the centre area or section of the quilt first and then work out from the centre. Anchor the layers of the quilt by quilting in the ditch between blocks and sashes of a patchwork quilt. Quilt the sashes before the blocks and quilt the areas of heavy stitching last.

Make sure the quilt is supported at all times and doesn't fall off the table and hang down, as this will cause the layers to shift and create distortion. End each line of stitching with a few stitches taken in place. After stitching each line, use a hand needle to thread the tails of thread and pull them into the middle of the quilting sandwich. Trim so that no thread shows on the surface.

Straight Line Quilting

For straight line machine quilting, use a walking foot (also called a 'dual feed' or 'even feed' foot) on your sewing machine. This will make it easier to quilt without causing puckers on the back of the quilt. Pull the bobbin thread to the surface by hand- turning the wheel of your machine. Make one revolution and stop with the needle in the highest position. Pull on the needle thread gently until the bobbin thread is pulled to the surface. Take several stitches in place to secure the beginning of the line of stitching. Hold the threads away from the stitching to prevent a snarl up.

Stitch in a slow and continuous manner, trying to avoid quick starts and stops. Do not tug or pull on the quilt sandwich while stitching but guide the fabric by positioning the hands on either side of the presser foot. Gently press down and hold the fabric taut to prevent puckers from occurring. If you gently spread your hands apart at either side of the fabric going though the machine you can maintain the tautness. Lift the presser foot and turn the quilt sandwich when necessary. Re-roll and fold the quilt to make it fit under the machine.

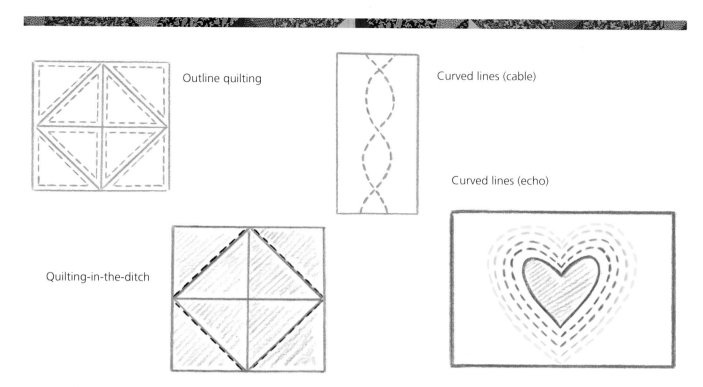

Outline quilting

Curved lines (cable)

Curved lines (echo)

Quilting-in-the-ditch

Outline quilting

This is quilting done .75 cm (¼ in) from the seam. It also defines each patch and helps to give a less puffy version with a little more texture than quilting-in-the-ditch. To mark a .75 cm (¼ in) quilting outline use .75 cm (¼ in) wide masking tape. To do this, lay the tape right next to the seam, and quilt next to the tape. Pull off the tape and lay it on the next seam. When this piece of tape wears out, use a new one. Do not leave the tape on the quilt when you are not quilting, or you may get a sticky build up.

Other forms of quilting are used to fill large areas where there is no piecing, for example in alternating plain blocks or on unpieced borders. These can be background grids of evenly spaced lines of quilting, or elaborate designs such as feathers and wreathes.

Quilting-in-the-ditch

If the quilting is done along the seam lines it is called quilting-in-the-ditch. When pressed, the seam allowances all lay on one side of the seam. When quilting-in-the-ditch, quilt on the side where there are no seam allowances. If you quilt on the wrong side, you will be quilting through four layers of fabric.

Quilting-in-the-ditch basically hides your stitches. If you are a beginner at hand-quilting this may be the option for you. Machine quilting-in-the-ditch can also be used. Quilting-in-the-ditch causes each patch to puff up

a bit and helps to define it. Another advantage of quilting-in-the-ditch is that no marking of the quilting design is needed. This not only saves time but also the worry of removing the marked line later. The only problem with quilting-in-the-ditch is it tends to leave large, open, unquilted areas in the larger patches.

Quilted grids

Straight lines are also used as background filler designs. Many quilts use a grid of diamonds, lines, or squares to fill large unpieced areas.

Pre-programmed embroidery stitches available on many sewing machines can be used instead of the straight stitch on long, straight lines of quilting.

Curved line quilting

These can be used to great effect. The elaborate cable and feather designs were popular in the past and used on unpieced borders or alternating plain blocks, which you can also do. Curved lines can also be used to fill background areas or to echo quilt, which outlines the motif several times. All curved lines are quilted on the machine with a technique called free motion quilting. Using free motion quilting enables you to create curved quilting designs with ease.

Continuous line quilting motifs designed to be sewn on the machine can be used to quilt blocks and borders. For this technique, cover or lower the dog feed and use

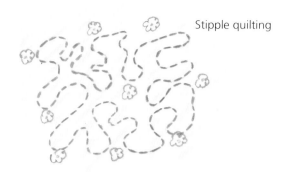

Stipple quilting

a darning foot. You must use you hands to move the quilt, as the dog feeds will no longer be feeding the quilt into the machine. The stitch length is determined by the speed of the machine and the movement of the quilt. Try to maintain a steady rhythm to maintain a uniform stitch length.

Stipple quilting

Use this technique for filling an area by using small meandering stitches in a random pattern. Stipple quilting was traditionally done quite close together to give a very prominent, puckery texture.

To achieve the appearance of stipple quilting, use a free motion quilting technique. To do this, first drop the dog feed and use the darning foot. Work in small sections and sew a meandering line in the area you are quilting. Leave yourself a place to escape from one area to the next if you don't want the stitching lines to cross. Try to cover the area evenly, using your hands to move the quilt beneath the needle.

HOW TO MAKE TIED QUILTS

Tying is a quick and easy way to finish a quilt. Many everyday quilts were traditionally finished off using this easy method. You can tie by hand or machine.

Embroidery thread or yarn can be used to hand-tie. Use cotton thread to machine-tie.

Hand-tied quilts

You can hand-tie instead of basting and quilting. Stretch the quilt sandwich as for basting and begin tying. To do this, use embroidery thread or yarn and a needle with an eye large enough for the thread or yarn to pass through without fraying. Leave a tail of thread hanging to tie later. Insert the needle through the layers and return to the surface, Make two back stitches. Return to the surface. Leave extra thread and move to the next spot to tie. Make two backstitches and travel to the next spot. Leave extra thread between each set of backstitches. Continue until you run out of thread. Clip the thread between the sets of backstitches in half and tie a square knot to finish. To make a square knot, tie the right thread over the left thread and then the left over the right. Pull tightly and trim all the tails to a uniform length. Ties can be spaced about 10cm (4 in) apart.

Machine-tied quilts

With this method there are no threads loose on the surface. Instead, the zigzag stitch holds the quilt in position and the hanging ends are tucked away inside the quilt.

To machine tie, first baste the quilt sandwich with safety pins. Use a table to support the weight of the quilt as you would for machine quilting. Roll up the side of the quilt that goes under the machine. Use a zigzag foot and a zigzag stitch to secure the layers. Stitch eight to ten times. Travel to the next area without cutting the thread. Leave enough thread between each tie to cut in half and thread into a hand needle. When the tying is finished, clip the thread between each tie. Thread into a needle and tuck the tails away inside the quilt batting.

Tying quilts

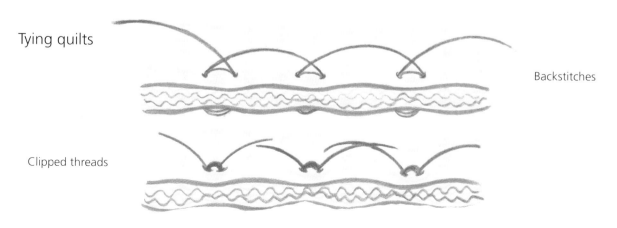

Backstitches

Clipped threads

FINISHING TECHNIQUES

Having completed your quilt top and assembled the batting and backing, you now need to bind the edges. These can be either a self-binding, an attached binding or an attractive triangular finish called prairie points. You may want to add your own style of border such as a frill or a fringe. These you would do as for normal sewing techniques and so are not covered here. You may want to display your quilt, rather than use it. If so, you will need to attach a hanging sleeve, which is explained at the end of this chapter.

◆

Self-binding finish

A self-binding is made with the backing fabric, which should be cut 1.5 cm (½ in) wider than the quilt top and batting. The backing fabric is brought round from the back, over the batting and quilt top and is then stitched into place, having first turned over a .75 cm (¼ in) hem.

Mitring corners

The corners on the self-bound finish are mitred, following the step by step diagrams below.

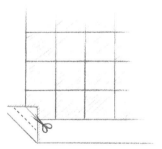

1. Fold corner of the backing at a 45° angle to the corner of the quilt.

2. Tuck the corner of the binding in until it touches the first fold. Press.

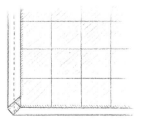

3. Fold edge in half, covering .75 cm (¼ in) allowance. Mitred corner has now been formed.

Attached binding finish

1 To attach a .75 cm (¼ in) binding, cut the strips 5 cm (2 in) on the straight of grain. To determine the total length of the strip, add up the measurement of all four sides of your quilt and add at least 45 cm (18 in) for overlapping the edges.

2 Join the strips together on the diagonal. Trim the seam allowance and press the seam open **(fig 1)**.

fig 1

3 On the starting end of the binding, cut a 45° angle. Fold under a .75 cm (¼ in) seam allowance and press. Fold the binding in half, with the right sides out, and press.

4 Lay the quilt right side up. Choose a starting point and place the binding on top of the quilt with both raw edges of the binding lined up with the raw edge of the quilt. Run the binding loosely around the edge of the quilt. Make sure no seams fall at the corners. If they do, Adjust your starting point. Leave the first 10 cm (4 in) of the binding unattached and begin sewing .75 cm (¼ in) in the middle of the top edge. It isn't necessary to pin. Sew slowly and stop stitching .75 cm (¼ in) from the corner **(fig 2)**. Remove the quilt from the machine and turn the quilt to the next side.

fig 2

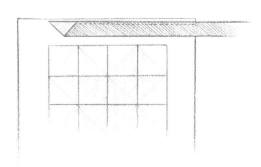

fig 4

fig 5

5 Fold the binding strip 90° away from the quilt. This creates a 45° angle **(fig 4)**. Fold binding back down with the new fold level with the raw edge of the quilt. This will make a mitred corner in reverse **(fig 5)**. Start stitching at the top edge and stop .75 cm (¼ in) from the next corner. Repeat the procedure for the other corners of the quilt.

6 When you are about 7.5 cm (8 in) from your starting point, remove the quilt from the sewing machine. Trim the end of the binding so that there is enough to finish the edge, plus 2.5 cm (1 in). Blindstitch the remaining binding to the edge of the quilt. When the two ends of the binding meet, tuck in the tail and continue to sew 2.5 cm (1 in) over the seamed 45° angle of the start of the binding. This will give you a neat join.

7 Fold the folded edge of the binding to the back of the quilt to cover the raw edges. Use a blindstitch to secure the binding to the back of the quilt. Be careful not to sew all the way through to the front or your stitches will show. When you come to the corner, you will find that a perfect mitre has formed on the front of the binding.

CONTINUOUS PRAIRIE POINT BORDERS
This is a great way to finish off the edges of your quilt. Traditionally, every square would have been folded separately and sewn in place but this quick method really cuts down the time needed to add a smart finish to your quilt.

1 Begin with two strips of fabric the length of the border it will be sewn to. The points will end up about half the width of the strips. Choose a width that divides evenly into the measurement of the border. For example, ten 30 cm (1 ft) squares, when folded into triangles, makes ten 15 cm (6 in) deep triangles. You can fudge up to 2.5 cm (1 in) if necessary by cutting off the last few points from the strip and spacing them to get the corner right.

2 Sew the two strips together with the wrong sides facing, offsetting the strips by half the width of the eventual triangle **(fig 1)**. Press open and place on the ironing board with the right sides down. The strips should then be cut into squares by cutting up to the seam line **(fig 2)**.

fig 1

fig 2

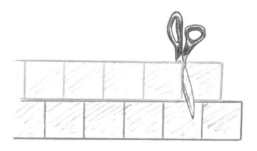

3 Fold the top right corner of the square of fabric 1 diagonally in half to form a triangle **(fig 3)**.

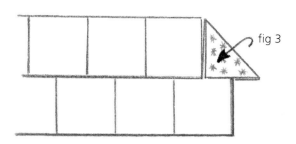

fig 3

4 Fold the top left point of the triangle diagonally down, until it is level with the seam. This forms one prairie point **(fig 4)**.

5 Repeat the above sequence with the corresponding square of fabric 2 **(figs 5 and 6)**. Fold over this triangle to overlay on the first triangle. The loose point on the first triangle comes outside the second triangle. Then flip the triangles away from strip 1. This frees the fabric for triangle 3 **(fig 7)**. Continue folding and marking triangles until you have sufficient triangles to fit the quilt edges.

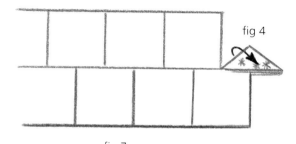

fig 4

fig 5

fig 6

fig 7

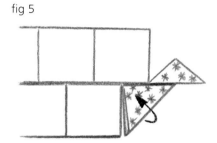

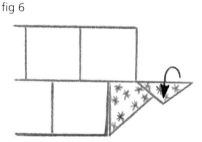

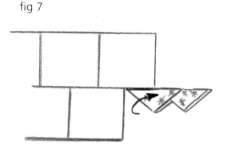

6 To attach the points, lay the prairie point strips on top of the right side of the quilt and sew with a .75 cm (¼ in) seam. Trim the backing to 1.5 cm (½ in) **(fig 8)**. Turn points out **(fig 9)**. Cover the raw edges with the backing and turn under. Blindstitch into place.

fig 9

fig 8

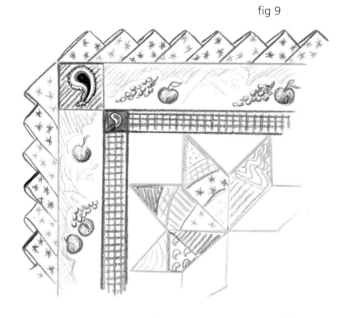

◆ DISPLAYING YOUR QUILT

After all that hard work, you will want your quilt to be admired by as many people as possible. Quilters often display their non-functional, more decorative quilts by hanging them on the wall. To do this attach a hanging sleeve after binding your quilt.

◆

MAKING A HANGING SLEEVE

1 Cut an 21.5 cm (8½ in) wide strip of calico the width of the quilt **(fig 1)**. Turn both the ends under by .75 cm (¼ in) and hem the short ends **(fig 2).**

fig 1

fig 2

2 Fold the sleeve fabric lengthways, with right sides facing together. Stitch a .75 cm (¼ in) seam along the length **(fig 3)**.

fig 3

3 Turn out to right side to form a tube and press. Lay the tube along the back of the quilt top. Blindstitch the top and the bottom of the tube into place **(fig 4)**.

fig 4

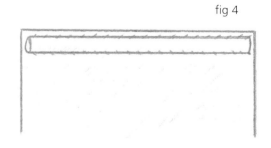

4 Once the sleeve has been attached, thread a length of doweling or a fancy curtain rod through and hang up on the wall.

THE PROJECTS

◆

IRIS SAMPLER PICNIC CLOTH

◆ *Quilt size: 120 x 120 cm (48 x 48 in)*

This little sampler picnic quilt would also look great as a wall hanging. Part of the fun of quiltmaking is learning to assemble and combine different patterns, which this quilt does. This is probably why sampler quilts are so popular, because you make each block only once, instead of making the same block several times. With this quilt you get the chance to sample nine different blocks – and to try out many of the techniques modern quiltmakers use to speed up the quilt-making process.

Many of the blocks used in the quilt are old favourites – the Rolling Star, Sawtooth Star and Nine Patch blocks. During the 1920s and 1930s these patterns were often printed in American newspapers for women readers to copy.

FABRIC QUANTITIES

1 ◆ **YELLOW PRINT**: 50 cm (½ yd)
2 ◆ **YELLOW AND BLUE PRINT**: 31.5 cm x 31.5 cm (12 ½ x 12 ½ in)
3 ◆ **BLUE SKY PRINT**: 25 cm (¼ yd)
4 ◆ **LIGHT IRIS PRINT**: 25 cm (¼ yd)
5 ◆ **ROYAL BLUE SOLID**: 25 cm (¼ yd)
6 ◆ **DARK IRIS PRINT**: 135 cm (1 ⅜ yd)
7 ◆ **GREEN SOLID**: 25 cm (¼ yd)
8 ◆ **MEDIUM BLUE CHINTZ**: 25 cm (¼ yd)
9 ◆ **YELLOW SOLID**: 35 cm (⅜ yd)
10 ◆ **MEDIUM BLUE PRINT**: 25 cm (¼ yd)
11 ◆ **MEDIUM BLUE SOLID**: 25 cm (¼ yd)
12 ◆ **ORANGE**: 5 cm x 5 cm (2 x 2 in)
13 ◆ **BACKING**: 130 x 130 cm (52 x 52 in) yellow solid
   ◆ **BATTING**: 130 x 130 cm (52 x 52 in)

ADDITIONAL MATERIALS

◆ **FREEZER PAPER**: for templates.

Key to sampler blocks

A Sawtooth Star (4 patch)
B Nine Patch (4 patch)
C Rolling Star (9 patch)
D Birds in the Air (4 patch)
E Iris Block
F Shoo Fly (9 patch)
G 54-40 or Fight (4 patch)
H Bear's Paw (9 patch)
I Ohio Star (9 patch)

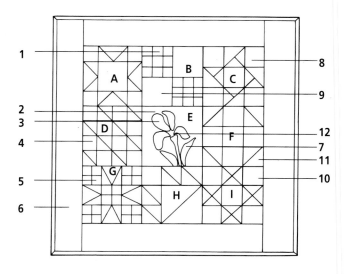

CUTTING INSTRUCTIONS

SAWTOOTH STAR: Cut one 18.5 cm (7 ¼ in) square of fabric 3. Cut across both diagonals, creating four quarter square triangles.
Cut four 10 cm (3 ⅞ in) squares of fabric 9. Cut across both diagonals, creating eight quarter square triangles.
Cut one 16.5 cm (6 ½ in) square of fabric 5.
Cut four 9 cm (3 ½ in) squares of fabric 4.

BIRDS IN THE AIR: Cut eight 9 cm (3 ½ in) squares of fabric 4.
Cut four 10 cm (3 ⅞ in) square of fabric 5. Cut across one diagonal, creating eight half square triangles.
Cut four 10 cm (3 ⅞ in) squares of fabric 9.

Cut across one diagonal, creating eight half square triangles.

54-40 OR FIGHT: Cut four shapes for template S1 from fabric 10.
Cut four shapes of template S2 from fabric 4. Cut four shapes of template S2 (reversed) from fabric 4.
Cut one strip 6.5 x 65 cm (2 ½ x 25 in) from fabric 5.
Cut one strip 6.5 cm x 65 cm (2 ½ x 25 in) from fabric 1.

NINE PATCH: Cut two 16.5 cm (6 ½ in) squares of fabric 9.
Cut one strip 6.5 x 60 cm (2 ½ x 24 in) of fabric 1. Cut into a 30 cm (12 in) strip and

two 15 cm (6 in) strips.
Cut one strip 6.5 x 75 cm (2 ½ x 28 in) of fabric 5. Cut into two 30 cm (12 in) strips and one 15 cm (6 in) strip.

IRIS BLOCK: Cut one 31.5 cm (12 ½ in) square of fabric 2.

Iris templates: Place the freezer paper shiny side down and iron to the wrong side of the fabric. Cut around the freezer paper shapes, allowing a .75 cm (¼ in) seam allowance. Use the glue stick to baste the seam allowance to the wrong side of the freezer paper pattern. Cut out two leaves and one stem from fabric 7, using templates S3, S4 and S5 on page 118.

PIECING INSTRUCTIONS

Make one block each of the following:

Sawtooth Star:

1 Sew the long side of two triangles of fabric 9 to each short side of a triangle of fabric 3. Repeat to make four flying geese units in all.

2 Join two of the flying geese units to the large middle square of fabric 5.

Sawtooth Star

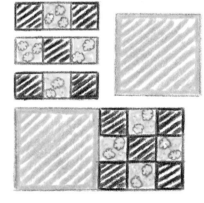

Nine Patch

3 Sew a square of fabric 4 to each end of the remaining two flying geese units. Sew the rows together.

Nine Patch:

1 Sew a 30 cm (12 in) strip of fabric 1 between two 30 cm (12 in) strips of fabric 5. Cut into four 6.5 cm (2 ½ in) strips **(fig 1)**.

2 Sew a 15 cm (6 in) strip of fabric 5 between two 15 cm (6in) strips of fabric 1. Cut into two 6.5 cm (2 ½ in) strips **(fig 2)**. Join the strips into two nine patch units **(fig 3)**.

fig 2

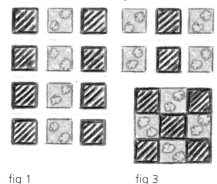

fig 1   fig 3

3 Sew a nine patch unit to a square of fabric 9 to make a row. Repeat and sew the two rows together, as shown in the diagram.

Cut out the 4 petals from fabric 3, using templates S6, S7, S8 and S9 (page 118). Cut the yellow of the iris centre from fabric 12, using template S10 (page 118).

BEAR'S PAW: Cut one 22.5 cm (8 ⅞ in) square of fabric 1. Cut on the diagonal, to make 2 half square triangles. (Use only one). Cut one 22.5 cm (8 ⅞ in) square of fabric 3. Cut on the diagonal, creating 2 half square triangles. (Use only one).

.Cut two 12.5 cm (4 ⅞ in) squares of fabric 9. Cut on one diagonal, creating 4 half square triangles.

Cut two 12.5 cm (4 ⅞ in) squares of fabric 5. Cut on one diagonal, creating four half square triangles.

Cut one 11.5 cm (4 ½ in) square of fabric 9.

ROLLING STAR: Cut four 11.5 cm (4 ½ in) squares of fabric 8.

Cut two 12.5 cm (4 ⅞ in) squares of fabric 3. Cut across one diagonal, creating four half square triangles.

Cut one 11.5 cm (4 ½ in) square of fabric 1. Cut one 13.5 cm (5 ¼ in) square of fabric 1. Cut across both diagonals, creating four quarter square triangles.

Cut one 13.5 cm (5 ¼ in) square of fabric 6. Cut across both diagonals, creating four quarter square triangles.

OHIO STAR: Cut four 11.5 cm (4 ½ in) squares of fabric 10.

Cut one 13.5 cm (5 ¼ in) square of fabric 3. Cut across both diagonals, creating four quarter square triangles.

Cut two 13.5 cm (5 ¼ in) squares of fabric 1. Cut across both diagonals, creating eight quarter square triangles.

Cut one 11.5 cm (4 ½ in) square of fabric 8. Cut one 13.5 cm (5 ¼ in) square of fabric 6. Cut across both diagonals, creating four quarter square triangles.

SHOO FLY: Cut one 11.5 cm (4 ½ in) square of fabric 1.

Cut four 11.5 cm (4 ½ in) squares of fabric 4. Cut two 12.5 cm (4 ⅞ in) squares of fabric 11. Cut across one diagonal, creating 4 half square triangles.

Cut two 12.5 cm (4 ⅞ in) of fabric 1. Cut across one diagonal, creating 4 half square triangles.

BORDER: Cut two 91.5 x 16.5 cm (36½ x 6½ in) strips of fabric 6. Cut two 121.5 x 16.5 cm (48½ x 6½ in) strips of fabric 6.

Rolling Star:

1 Sew the quarter square triangle units from the triangles of fabric 1 and fabric 6. Make four units.

2 Sew the quarter square triangle units to the half triangles of fabric 3 to form a square.

3 Sew into rows, with squares of fabric 8 and fabric 1, as shown in the diagram.

Birds in the Air:

1 Join the eight half square triangles of fabrics 5 and 9 to form squares. Join these pieced squares to the squares of fabric 4, alternating as shown in the diagram.

Iris Block:

1 Pin the shapes to the 31.5 cm (12 ½ in) block of fabric 3. Blindstitch into place.

2 Trim away the fabric beneath the applied shapes. Dampen the freezer paper and gently tug to remove the templates.

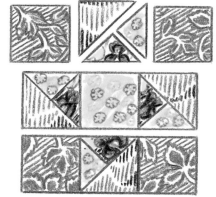

Rolling Star

Birds in the Air

Iris Block

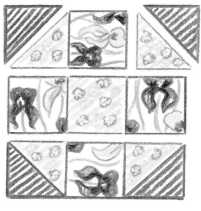

Shoo Fly

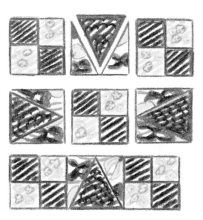

54-40 or Fight

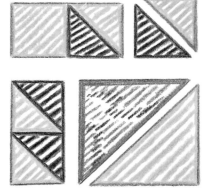

Bear's Paw

Ohio Star

Shoo Fly:

1 Make four half square triangle units from the triangles of fabric 1 and 11.

2 Assemble these units with the four squares of fabrics 4 and one square of fabric 1 into rows, as shown in the diagram.

54-40 or Fight:

1 Sew the strip of fabric 5 to the strip of fabric 1. Cut the pieced strip to make ten 6.5 cm (2 ½ in) strips.

2 Join two of the pieced strips into a four patch unit. Make four other four patch units.

3 Sew one S1 triangle of fabric 10 to one S2 triangle of fabric 4 **(fig 1)**.

fig 1

4 Sew a reversed S2 triangle to the other side of the large S1 triangle. Make four units **(fig 1)**.

5 Join the patches into rows and join the rows together, as shown in the diagram.

Bear's Paw:

1 Join a triangle of fabric 9 to a triangle of fabric 5. Make four units. Join the triangle of fabric 1 to the triangle of fabric 3. Sew into rows and then sew the rows together.

Ohio Star:

1 Sew the quarter square triangles of fabric 1 and 3 together. Sew the quarter square triangles of fabric 6 and 1 together. Sew the pieced triangles units together to form four squares.

2 Assemble these units with the four squares of fabric 10 and one square of fabric eight in rows, as shown in the diagram.

Quilt assembly

Assembly Instructions

1 Sew the blocks together into rows. Sew the rows together, following the assembly diagram.

2 Add the side border panels. Add the top and bottom border panels.

3 Sandwich the quilt top with the batting and backing fabric. Pin and baste. Quilt the quilt top using stipple, quilting-in-the-ditch, outline and curved lines. Trim top and batting and then self-bind with the backing fabric.

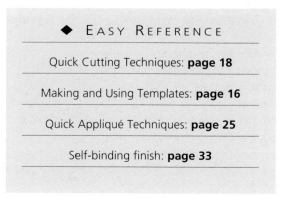

◆ Easy Reference

Quick Cutting Techniques: **page 18**

Making and Using Templates: **page 16**

Quick Appliqué Techniques: **page 25**

Self-binding finish: **page 33**

COUNTRY KITCHEN ACCESSORIES

Patchwork kitchen accessories can really personalise your kitchen. This set of four placemats, tea cosy and table mat would spice up any traditional or contemporary country kitchen. Using various different country animal prints in cream, red and black give these kitchen accessories their special flavour. Choose a few fabrics with the same theme. A large scale print is great for the centre of the placemats, while small or medium-scale prints work best for the smaller triangular patches. The placemats can be made up very quickly using the rotary cutting and grid method for making the triangles. Who knows, you could be enjoying a country breakfast tomorrow morning!

FABRIC QUANTITIES AND CUTTING INSTRUCTIONS

1 ◆ CREAM PRINT WITH COWS: 75 cm (¾ yd)
Cut three strips 9 cm (3 ½ in wide). Cut twenty 9 cm (3 ½ in) squares from strips. Cut one rectangle 80 x 40 cm (32 x 16 in) to make the grid triangles.

2 ◆ RED PRINT WITH CHICKENS: 50 cm (½ yd)
Cut one rectangle 80 x 40 cm (32 x 16 in).

3 ◆ RED PRINT WITH COWS: 35 cm (½ yd)
Cut nine strips 4 (1 ½ in) wide from the fabric width. Cut these into eight strips 31.5 cm (12 ½ in) long, eight strips 51.5 cm (20 ½ in) long, two strips 24 cm (9 ½ in) long and two strips 29 cm (11 ½ in). They should all be 4 cm (1 ½ in) wide.

4 ◆ BLACK & WHITE PRINT: 2.20 m (3 ⅜ yd)
Cut nine strips 6 cm (2 in) wide from the width of the fabric for binding.

5 ◆ LARGE SCALE ANIMAL PRINT 50 cm (½ yd)
Cut four 31.5 x 16.5 cm (12 ½ x 6 ½ in) rectangles.
Cut two rectangles 24 x 39.25 cm (9 ½ x 15 ½ in).
Cut one 9 cm (3 ½ in) square for tablemat.

◆ BATTING: 76 x 76 in (190 x 190 cm)
Two rectangles 35 x 42.5 cm (14 x 17 in).
One 30 cm (12 in) square.
Four rectangles 55 x 40 cm (22 x 16 in).

For backings: Cut two rectangles 35 x 42.5 cm (14 x 17 in) and one 30 cm (12 in) square (tea cosy).
Cut four rectangles 55 x 40 cm (22 x 16 in) (table mat).
Cut four rectangles 55 x 40 cm (22 x 16 in) (place mats).

Key to fabrics

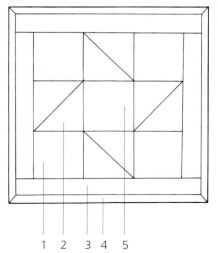

1   2   3 4   5

PIECING INSTRUCTIONS

1 Make 64 fast half square triangle units from fabrics by using the 85 x 40 cm (32 x 16 in) rectangles of fabrics 1 and 2. Mark a 4 x 8 grid of squares measuring 10 x 10 cm (3 $\frac{7}{8}$ x 3 $\frac{7}{8}$ in) each (see grid diagram). Draw diagonal lines through the corners of the squares going in one direction.

2 Use 48 of these squares to make the four placemats, 10 squares for the tea cosy and four squares to make the table mat.

Grid diagram

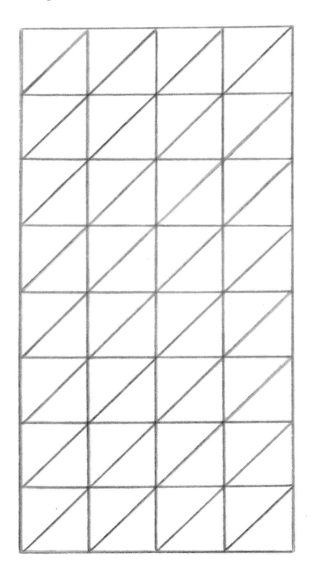

PIECING AND ASSEMBLY INSTRUCTIONS

Placemats and table mat:

1 Sew the patches together into rows and then sew the rows together to complete the top of the placemat [see assembly diagram].

2 Press the seams flat. Layer with batting and backing fabric. You may wish to use a double layer of batting for the table mat.

3 Sew the top of the quilt across the triangles and continuing right across the piece using the quilting-in-the-ditch technique.

4 Bind the edges of the table mat and placemats with 6 cm (2 in) strips of fabric 4.

Tea cosy:

1 Sew together five of the prepared half square triangle units. Make another strip in the same way. Sew one strip to each piece of the large animal print. Press.

2 Layer each piece with a layer of batting and backing and baste. Machine quilt on the diagonal.

3 Make an enlarged pattern of the tea cosy template CK1 on page 124 (1 grid square = 7.5 cm (3 in)). Place 2 quilted pieces, right sides together, and attach to the pieces. Cut around the pattern. Sew a small 5 cm x 2.5 cm (2 x 1 in) scrap into a tube and turn right side out. Place at the top of the curve between the right sides of the tea cosy **(fig 1)**. Stitch along the curved edge with a .75 cm (¼ in) seam allowance. Clip the curve. Bind the open edge with 6 cm (2 in) strips of fabric.

fig 1

Turn to the front

Placemat assembly

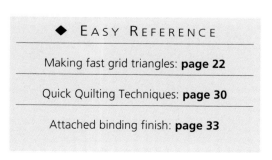

Tablemat assembly

Tea cosy assembly

◆ EASY REFERENCE

Making fast grid triangles: **page 22**

Quick Quilting Techniques: **page 30**

Attached binding finish: **page 33**

OHIO STAR QUILT

◆ *Quilt size: 180 x 210 cm (72 x 84 in)*

Ablue and white quilt makes a soothing and peaceful addition to any bedroom. The Liberty lawn cottons lend a special quality to the quilt and are very soft to the touch. Add a blue print and a green print to the Liberty florals and you're off to a good start and adding the patterned border creates a very professional finishing touch.

This is a surprisingly easy quilt to make and uses two traditional alternating blocks – the Ohio Star and the Snowball. This latter block is often used instead of a plain alternating block to create a star frame around its companion block. Combining the Ohio Star and the Snowball creates a dramatic double star effect.

FABRIC QUANTITIES AND CUTTING INSTRUCTIONS

1 ◆ DARK BLUE PRINT: 1 m (1 yd)
Cut thirty 13.5 cm (5 ¼ in) squares and cut across both diagonals, creating 120 quarter square triangles.

2 ◆ LARGE SCALE BLUE & WHITE PRINT: 180 cm (2 yds)
Cut twelve 31.5 cm (12 ½ in) squares.

3 ◆ LIGHT BLUE SOLID: 90 cm (1 yard)
Cut forty-eight 11.5 cm (4 ½ in) squares.

4 ◆ GREEN PRINT: 50 cm (½ yd)
Cut fifteen 13.5 cm (5 ¼ in) squares. Cut on both diagonals, creating 60 quarter square triangles.

5 ◆ SMALL SCALE BLUE AND WHITE: 165 cm (1 ⅝ yd)
Cut sixty 11.5 cm (4 ½ in) squares. Cut

fifteen 13.5 cm (5 ¼ in) squares. Cut on both diagonals, creating 60 quarter square triangles.

6 ◆ MEDIUM SCALE BLUE AND WHITE PRINT: 35 cm (⅜ yd)
Cut fifteen 1.5 cm (4 ½ in) squares.

7 ◆ BORDER PRINT: 225 cm (2 ⅝ yd)
Cut two border panels 195 x 16.5 cm (78 x 6 ½in).
Cut two border panels 225 x 16.5 cm (90 x 6 ½in).

8 ◆ BACKING: 205 x 225 cm (2 ½ yds x 90 in)
Cut a 190 x 220 cm (76 x 88 in) backing.

◆ BATTING: 190 x 220 cm (76 x 88 in)

Key to fabrics

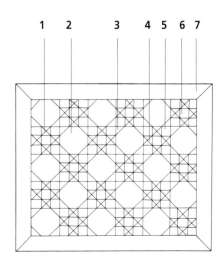

PIECING INSTRUCTIONS

Ohio Star Block:

1 Sew the triangles of fabrics 1, 4 and 5 together to form one square, following the positioning sequence in **fig 1.** Make four.

fig 1

2 Using a square of fabric 6 and four squares of fabric 5, follow the sequence of **fig 2** to assemble a block. Make fifteen blocks in this way.

fig 2

Snowball Block:

1 Place a square of fabric 3 in one corner of a large square of fabric 2. Draw a line across the diagonal of fabric 3 and sew on the line **(fig 3).** Trim both layers .75 m (¼ in) from the seam. Press the seam to one side.

fig 3

2 Repeat the same steps for each corner. The block should now have 4 triangles at each corner **(fig 4).** Make twelve blocks in this way.

fig 4

ASSEMBLY INSTRUCTIONS

1 Sew the rows together (5 rows x 6 rows) in an alternating pattern, as shown on the assembly diagram. Add the border panels, mitring the corners.

2 Press the quilt top. Layer the quilt sandwich with the quilt top, batting and backing. Pin and baste.

3 Quilt by using the quilting-in-the-ditch technique along diagonal, horizontal and vertical seams.

4 Trim the batting even with the top and then self-bind the quilt with the backing fabric.

Assembly of the quilt

◆ EASY REFERENCE

Cutting quarter square triangles: **page 19**

Mitring corners: **page 33**

Quick Quilting Techniques: **page 30**

Self-binding finish: **page 33**

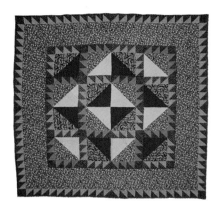

DELECTABLE MOUNTAINS QUILT

◆ *Quilt size: 180 x 180 cm (72 x 72 in)*

This traditional pattern gives the impression of looking down onto the peak of a mountain. The lovely rich tones of the red, green and gold paisleys chosen for my version show how simple it is to create a quilt that radiates a warm glow in the most stylish of ways. This quilt isn't as complicated as it might at first look, particularly if you use the grid method for making fast half square triangles. All the patches are quick-cut, using a rotary cutter.

The quilt is made from one four-patch block. Block A and B are the same, except different fabrics are used. The blocks alternate and are also rotated so that a medallion-type arrangement of triangles inside squares appears. The medallion is completed with a plain inner border and a pieced sawtooth border on the outer edge.

Straight line quilting is used on the quilt top to give it a wonderful texture.

FABRIC QUANTITIES AND CUTTING INSTRUCTIONS

1 ◆ GOLD: 30 cm (⅓ yd)
Cut four squares 25 cm (9⅞ in). Cut across one diagonal to make 8 half square triangles for Block A.

2 ◆ RED: 30 cm (⅓ yd)
Cut four squares 25 cm (9⅞ in). Cut across one diagonal to make 8 half square triangles for Block B.

3 ◆ RED/GOLD PRINT: 1.8 m (2 yd)
Cut two border strips 121.5 cm x 24 cm (48½ x 9½ in). Cut two border strips 166.5 cm x 24 cm (66½ x 9½ in). Cut four squares 25cm (9⅞ in). Cut across one diagonal to make 8 half square triangles for Block A.

4 ◆ RED DOT PRINT: 90 cm (1 yd)
Cut two rectangles 30 cm x 40 cm (12 x 16 in) for Block A quick triangles. Cut a rectangle 40 cm x 50 cm (16 x 20 in) for border triangles. Cut a rectangle 40 cm x 60 cm (16 x 24 in) for border triangles. Cut twelve 9 cm (3½ in) squares. Use 8 for Block A and use 4 for the sawtooth border posts.

5 ◆ YELLOW PRINT: 30 cm (⅓ yd)
Cut two rectangles 30 cm x 40 cm (12 x 16 in) for Block B triangles. Cut a rectangle 40 cm x 50 cm (16 x 20 in) for border triangles. Cut a rectangle 40 cm x 60cm (16 x 24 in) for border triangles.

6 ◆ GREEN/GOLD PAISLEY: 30 cm (⅓ yd)
Cut four squares 25 cm (9⅞ in). Cut across one diagonal to make 8 half square triangles for Block B.

7 ◆ GREEN PRINT: 30 cm (⅓ yd)
Cut two rectangles 30 cm x 40 cm(12 x 16 in) for Block A triangles.

8 ◆ GREEN PAISLEY: 90 cm (1 yd)
Cut two rectangles 30 cm x 40 cm (12 x 16 in) for Block B triangles. Cut eight 9 cm (3½ in) squares for Block B. Cut eight strips 6 cm x 110 cm (2 x 44 in) for binding.

◆ BACKING FABRIC: 3.8 m (4¼ yd)
Cut two pieces 190 cm x 105 cm (76 x 42 in) after removing selvedges.

◆ BATTING: 190 cm x 190 cm (76 x 76 in)

Key to fabrics

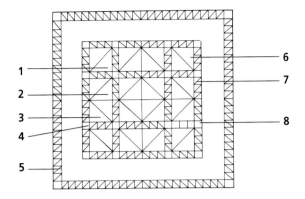

PIECING INSTRUCTIONS:

Block A:

1 Sew one triangle of fabric 1 to one triangle of fabric 3 to make the large square patch. Make eight squares in this way.

Block A triangles

1 Use the rectangles of fabrics 4 and 7 and cut a 30 cm x 40 cm (12 x 16 in) piece from each of the fabrics to make the Block A fast triangles.

2 On the wrong side of the top fabric, mark a 3 x 4 grid of squares measuring 10 cm (3 ⅞ in) each. This grid will make 24 finished squares measuring 7.5 cm (3 in).

Block A

3 Repeat with the remaining two 30 cm x 40cm (12 x 16 in) rectangles of fabrics 4 and 7. This makes 48 squares in total.

4 Follow the piecing diagram to assemble the block. Make eight blocks.

fig 2

Block B:

1 Sew one triangle of fabric 2 to one triangle of fabric 6 to make the large square patch. Make eight squares.

Block B triangles

1 Use the rectangles of fabrics 5 and 8 measuring 30 cm x 40cm (12 x 16 in) for Block B fast triangles. Make the triangles in the same way as for Block A triangles. Make 48 squares.

2 Follow the piecing diagram to assemble the block. Make eight blocks.

Block B

Border triangles

1 Use the rectangles of fabrics 4 and 5 measuring 40 cm x 50 cm (16 x 20 in) to make the fast border triangles.

2 Use a 4 x 5 grid of squares measuring 10 x 10 cm (3 ⅞ x 3 ⅞ in) each. Make 40 units. Repeat, using the remaining rectangles measuring 40 cm x 60 cm (16 x 24 in). Draw a 6 x 4 grid. This makes 48 squares. You should have 88 squares in total.

3 Sew 11 squares together to form half a border. Make four of these strips. Repeat, making four mirror image strips. Sew them together in pairs to make four borders **(fig 1)**.

fig 1

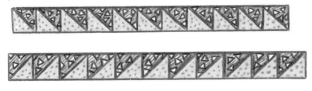

4 Sew the four corner squares (posts) of fabric 4 on each end of two of the strips **(fig 2)**.

5 Assemble the blocks into rows, as shown in the assembly diagram. Add the inner borders. Sew on the outer borders.

Assembly of the quilt

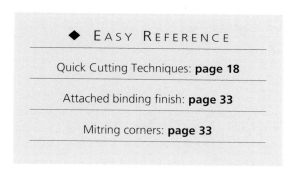

ASSEMBLY INSTRUCTIONS

1 Press the quilt top and mark the diagonal quilting design on the top. You can use .75 cm (¼ in) masking tape instead of marking the top with pencil.

2 Join the backing together. Layer the quilt sandwich with the quilt top, batting and backing. Pin and baste.

3 Machine quilt each quarter of the quilt on the diagonal, forming a chevron design.

4 Trim the backing, batting and quilt top so that they are even.

5 Bind the quilt by using the eight strips of fabric 8. Join them together on the diagonal and attach around the edge of the quilt, mitring the corners.

◆ EASY REFERENCE

Quick Cutting Techniques: **page 18**

Attached binding finish: **page 33**

Mitring corners: **page 33**

BUNNY QUILT

◆ *Quilt size: 170 x 230 cm (68 x 92 in)*

Stencilled bunnies frolic in a lush garden of veggies on this colourful quilt. When I saw these fabrics I knew I had to make a bunny rabbit quilt. I considered appliqué bunnies but decided that stencilling them onto the quilt would give it a country folk art appeal. It's really easy – and fun – to stencil with fabric paints.

Many country quilts from the 1930s were tied instead of quilted as it is a much faster way to finish off a quilt. My ten year-old daughter Kacy and my friend Colleen Ann Sharkey, intently watched by my son Perry, tied the quilt and left the threads fairly long to give a lovely grassy feel to the garden!

FABRIC QUANTITIES AND CUTTING INSTRUCTIONS

1 ◆ VEGETABLE PRINT MEDIUM: 125 cm (1¼ yd)
Cut twelve squares 17.5 cm (6 ⅞ in). Cut them on the diagonal to make 24 half square triangles. Cut six squares 32.5 cm (12 ⅞ in). Cut them on the diagonal to make 12 half square triangles.

2 ◆ VEGETABLE PRINT LIGHT: 125 cm (1¼ yd)
Cut twelve squares 17.5 cm (6 ⅞ in). Cut on one diagonal to make two half square triangles.
Cut six squares 32.5 cm (12 ⅞ in). Cut on one diagonal to make two half square triangles.

3 ◆ VEGETABLE PRINT DARK: 225 cm (2¼ yd)

Cut two strips 26.5cm x 181.5 cm (10 ½ in x 72 ½ in).
Cut two strips 26.5 x 171.5 cm (10 ½ in x 68 ½ in).

4 ◆ OFF WHITE COTTON: 75 cm (¾ yd)
Cut six 31.5 x 31.5 cm (12 ½ x 12 ½ in) squares.

5 ◆ BACKING: 180 x 240 cm (72 x 96 in)

◆ BATTING: 180 x 240 cm (72 x 96 in)

ADDITIONAL MATERIALS

◆ **FABRIC PAINT:** in brown, green and pearlised white.

◆ **KITCHEN SPONGE OR STENCIL BRUSH.**

◆ **STENCIL ACETATE:** for bunnies.

◆ **EMBROIDERY THREAD:** in green and yellow.

Key to fabrics

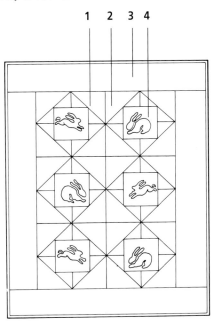

TEMPLATES AND STENCILLING

1 Using the bunny templates B1 and B2 on page 119 cut one stencil of each bunny with a craft knife. To stencil each bunny, place the stencil over a square of fabric 4 **(fig 1)**. You can use a dab of glue stick to hold down the stencil.

fig 1

2 Dab a dry brush or sponge into the brown paint. Blot off most of the paint onto a scrap of paper.

3 Sponge the paint into the bunny shape. Create depth by making the brown darker around the edges by dabbing over the edges more often than you dab in the centre of the shape **(fig 2)**. The green paint is used for the lettuce shape and the tails are painted with pearlised white paint.

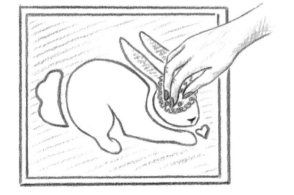

fig 2

4 Allow the bunny to dry before removing the stencil. Set the paint according to the instructions. Paint the other bunnies, making three of each stencil. The reversed bunnies are made by turning the stencil over.

PIECING INSTRUCTIONS

1 Sew one small triangle of fabric 1 to a small triangle of fabric 2 to make a larger triangle. Make twelve triangles with fabric 1 on the right side of the triangle **(fig 3)**. Make twelve triangles with fabric 2 on the right side of the triangle **(fig 4)**.

fig 3   fig 4

2 Sew the pieced triangles to the bunny squares. Sew the large corner triangles to each pieced unit **(fig 5)**. Sew the six bunny blocks together (see quilt assembly diagram opposite).

3 Attach the borders, sewing on the side strips first and then the top and bottom strips.

fig 5

Quilt assembly

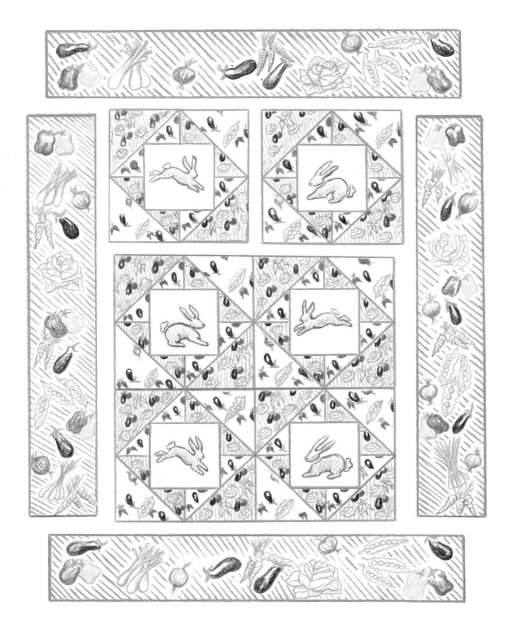

ASSEMBLY INSTRUCTIONS

1 Press the quilt top. Sandwich the quilt top with the batting and backing fabric. Pin and baste.

2 Use embroidery thread to sew a large running stitch around the edges of the bunnies and inside the bunny blocks. Tie the layers together with the embroidery thread. Trim the top and batting even and then self-bind with the backing fabric.

◆ EASY REFERENCE

Cutting half square triangles: **page 19**

Self-binding finish: **page 33**

Hand- and machine-tied quilts **page 32**

NINE PATCH AND HEARTS BABY QUILT

◆ *Quilt size: 94 x 115 cm (37½ x 46 in)*

There's nothing like a homemade quilt to welcome a new baby and this one is a quick and easy gift to make for the new arrival. The nine-patch block is very easy to do using strip piecing and rotary cutting techniques and the appliqué is a breeze if you use paper-backed fusible web and the zig-zag setting on your machine. The cross stitch pattern, designed by Colleen Ann Skarkey, adds cute little nappy pins and the word 'BABY'. Using waste canvas makes the cross stitch very simple to do. Machine quilting makes the quilt more durable, ensuring it will last a childhood of washings.

FABRIC QUANTITIES AND CUTTING INSTRUCTIONS

1 ◆ BLUE PRINT: 25 cm (⅜ yd)
Cut two 6.5 x 105 cm (2 ½ x 42 in) strips.
Cut one 6.5 x 80 cm (2 ½ x 32 in) strips.
Cut two 6.5 x 55 cm (2 ½ x 22 in) strips.

2 ◆ YELLOW PRINT: 25 cm (⅜ yd)
Cut one 6.5 x 105 cm (2 ½ x 42 in) strips.
Cut two 6.5 x 80 cm (2 ½ x 32 in) strips.
Cut one 6.5 x 55 cm (2 ½ x 32) strips.

3 ◆ MEDIUM BLUE SOLID: 50 cm (⅝ yd)
Cut three 24.5 cm (9 ¾ in) squares. Cut on both diagonals to make 12 triangles (2 will be spare).
Cut six 16.5 cm (6 ½ in) squares.
Cut two 13.75 cm (5 ⅛ in) squares. Cut across the diagonal to make 4 triangles.

4 ◆ PINK: 50 cm (25 cm (½ yd)
For heart templates (see page 62).

5 ◆ YELLOW BABY PRINT: 1 m (1 ⅛ yd)
Cut two 16.5 x 86.5 cm (6 ½ x 34 ½ in) border panels. Cut two 16.5 x 94 cm (6 ½ x 37 ½ in) border panels.

6 ◆ BLUE BABY PRINT (BACKING): 105 x 125 cm (42 x 50 in).

◆ **BATTING:** 105 x 125 cm (42 x 50 in)

ADDITIONAL MATERIALS
◆ **MACHINE EMBROIDERY THREAD:** in fuschia.
◆ **STRANDED COTTON:** lemon, yellow, blue.
◆ **WASTE CANVAS:** 12 in square with 10 holes per inch.
Cut six 7.5 cm (3 in) squares of waste canvas.
◆ **PAPER-BACKED FUSIBLE WEB:** for templates.

Key to fabrics

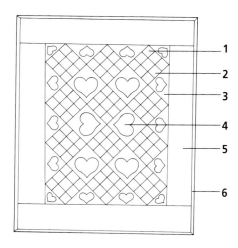

TEMPLATES

1 Make the heart templates by tracing round the template shapes on page 119 on the fusible web as follows:
6 x Heart template H1
10 x heart template H2
4 x Heart template H3

Press all the fusible web templates onto the wrong side of fabric 4. Cut out each heart.

PIECING INSTRUCTIONS

1 Sew one 6.5 x 105 cm (2 ½ x 42 in) of fabric 2 between two strips of the same length of fabric 1. Cut into sixteen 6.5 cm (2 ½ in) strips **(fig 1)**.

2 Sew one 6.5 x 80 cm (2 ½ x 32 in) of fabric 1 between two strips of the same length of fabric 2. Cut into twelve 6.5 cm (2 ½ in) strips **(fig 2)**.

3 Sew one 6.5 x 55 cm (2 ½ x 22 in) of fabric 2 between two strips of the same length of fabric 1. Cut into eight 6.5 cm (2 1½ in) strips **(fig 3)**. Make twelve nine-patch blocks from the sewn strips, assembling as shown **(fig 4)**.

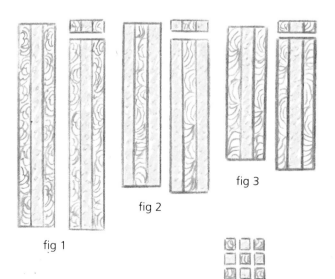

fig 3

fig 2

fig 1

fig 4

4 Using the fusible web, fuse the H1 hearts on to the 16.5 cm (6 ½ in) squares of fabric 3. Fuse the H2 hearts onto the larger triangles squares of fabric 3. Fuse the H3 hearts onto the smaller triangles squares of fabric 3 **(fig 5).**

fig 5

5 Thread the bobbin and needle with machine embroidery thread in fuschia. Set the machine to zigzag stitch with the stitch length very low to create a satin stitch. Sew around the edge of each heart. Pivot with the needle down at the valley and point of the hearts.

6 Place a square of waste canvas in the middle of each large heart. Pin into place. Cross stitch the BABY design with the stranded cotton, following the diagram on page 122. Loosen the waste canvas by dampening it with water. Remove each individual strand of canvas by gently tugging with tweezers.

7 Sew the blocks into rows, following the diagram (opposite).

Quilt assembly

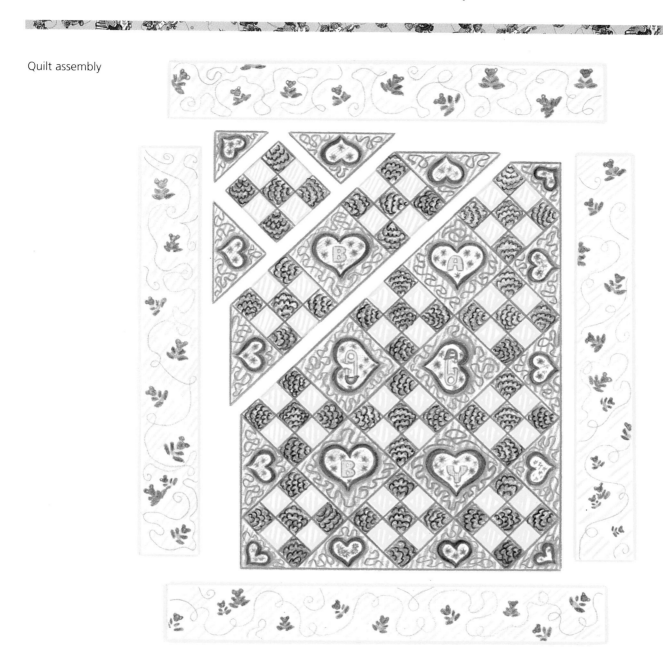

ASSEMBLY INSTRUCTIONS

1 Attach the borders of fabric 5 and press the quilt top.

2 Assemble the backing, batting and quilt top and then pin and baste.

3 Quilt by using the quilting-in-the-ditch stitch between the blocks. Stipple quilt around the hearts and use freestyle quilting around the border.

4 Trim the quilt top and backing and then self-bind with the backing fabric, mitring the corners.

◆ EASY REFERENCE

Quick Appliqué Techniques **page 25**

Quick Quilting Techniques **page 30**

Self-binding finish **page 33**

Mitring corners **page 33**

COUNTRY BASKET QUILT

◆ *Quilt size: 96 x 96 cm (38 x 38 in)*

This country quilt features a traditional basket pattern of flowers in a medallion setting. There are many traditional basket patterns but I chose this one because it has a large open triangle to fill with appliqué flowers but you could also fill it with fruit, which would look equally attractive. The golden brown ethnic fabric seemed to suggest basket weave so I decided to add it, and I thought the gold and brown fabrics provided a really traditional feel.

The quilt is very quick to make as it is pieced by machine using rotary cutting and strip piecing techniques.

FABRIC QUANTITIES AND CUTTING INSTRUCTIONS

1 ◆ BASKET PRINT: 50 cm (½ yd)
Cut two strips 6.5 cm x 76.5 cm
(2 ½ x 30 ½ in).
Cut two strips 6.5 cm x 66.5 cm
(2 ½ x 26 ½ in).
Cut two strips 6 cm x 47.5 cm (2 ¼ x 19 in).
Cut two strips 6 x 39.25 cm (2 ¼ x 15 ½ in).
Cut four 10 cm (3 ⅞ in) squares and cut on one diagonal.

2 ◆ BROWN PRINT: 50 cm (½ yd)
Cut nine 4 cm (1 ½ in) wide strips the width of the fabric. Cut out seven freezer paper patterns of template CB2.

3 ◆ LIGHT GOLD PRINT: 50 cm (½ yd)

Cut nine 4 cm (1 ½ in) wide strips the width of the fabric. Cut out seven freezer paper patterns using template CB1.

4 ◆ MEDIUM GOLD: 25 cm (¼ yd)
Cut out seven of the freezer paper patterns using template CB3.

5 ◆ BLUE WEAVE PRINT: 15 cm (¼ yd)
Cut five 10 cm (3 ⅞ in) squares and cut on one diagonal.

6 ◆ CREAM BACKGROUND: 65 cm (¾ yd)
Cut one square 51.5 cm (19 ¾ in) and cut on both diagonals. Cut one 32.5 cm (12 ⅞ in) square and cut one diagonal. Cut one 17.5 cm (6 ⅞ in) square and cut on one

diagonal. Cut two 7.5 cm x 22 cm (2 ½ x 9 ½ in) rectangles.

7 ◆ LIGHT GREEN: 15 cm (¼ yd)
Cut one 9 cm (3 ½ in) wide strip the width of the fabric.

8 ◆ DARK GREEN: 15 cm (¼ yd)
Cut one 6.5 cm (2 ½ in) wide strip the width of the fabric.

9 ◆ BACKING FABRIC: 100 x 100 cm
(42 x 42 in)

◆ **BATTING:** 100 x 100 cm (42 x 42 in)

ADDITIONAL EQUIPMENT
◆ FREEZER PAPER

Key to
fabrics

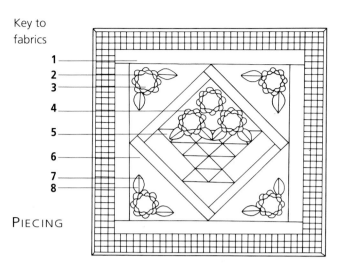

PIECING

INSTRUCTIONS

1 Make six half square triangles from the triangles of fabrics 1 and 5. Make one row of three units and sew a triangle of fabric 5 on the end. Make one row of two units and sew a triangle of fabric 5 at the end. Also sew a triangle of fabric 5 to one unit **(fig 1)**.

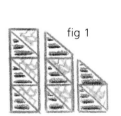

fig 1

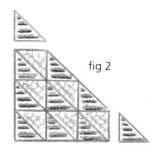

fig 2

2 Sew a triangle of fabric 5 to the half square triangle unit. Sew together in rows to form a triangle **(fig 2)**.

3 Sew to one of the medium-sized triangles of fabric 6 to make a square **(fig 3)**. The other triangle of fabric 6 is not needed.

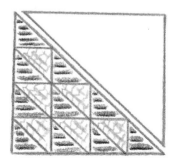

fig 3

4 Sew a triangle of fabric 1 to a rectangle of fabric 6. Make two. Sew the rectangle/triangle piece to the pieced square. Sew a small triangle of fabric 6 to the bottom of the basket to complete the central block **(fig 4)**.

fig 4

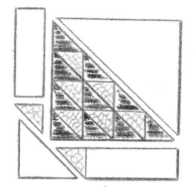

5 Add the first border of fabric 1. Add the four large triangles of fabric 6. Add the outer border of fabric 1 **(fig 5)**.

fig 5

fig 6

6 To make the chequerboards, sew the strips of fabrics 3 and 2 together in strips of three. Make two types of strips (fabrics 2, 3, 2 and fabric 3, 2, 3). **(fig 6)**.

7 Make three strip sets (strata) of each type. Cut the strata into 4 cm (1½ in) strips. Make twenty-two nine patch blocks of each type **(fig 7)**. Sew into border rows and attach as shown on the assembly diagram opposite.

fig 7

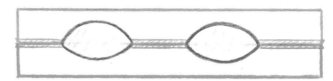

APPLIQUÉ

1 Sew the strips of fabrics 7 and 8 together. Press twelve freezer paper leaf templates CB4 (page 118) to wrong side of the strip, positioning the seam along the centre of the leaf. Cut around the patterns adding a .75 cm (¼ in) seam allowance **(fig 8).** Glue the seam allowance to the back of the pattern with a glue stick. Smooth out any wrinkles. Machine or hand appliqué with blind hemstitch to the appropriate triangles. Cut out the flowers using templates CB1, CB2 and CB3 from

fig 8

fabrics 2, 3 and 4 as indicated on Fabric Quantities and Cutting Instructions and apply them in the same way.

2 Trim excess layers from the back. Wet the freezer paper pattern and gently tug to remove.

Quilt assembly

ASSEMBLY INSTRUCTIONS

1 Press the quilt top. Layer the quilt sandwich with the quilt top, batting and backing. Baste.

2 Quilt the top using the outline quilting technique. Outline-quilt the four outer triangles and the inner creme coloured fabric. Echo quilt around all the flowers and leaves.

3 Trim the quilt top and back even and then self-bind with the backing fabric.

◆ EASY REFERENCE

Cutting half square triangles **page 19**

Strip pieced chequerboards **page 20**

Quick Appliqué Techniques **page 25**

Quick Quilting Techniques **page 30**

Self-binding finish: **page 33**

RAIL FENCE WALL HANGING

◆ *Quilt size: 90 x 120 cm (48 x 36 in)*

This traditional pattern is aptly named. The little rectangles form a square block that is rotated 90 degrees in alternate blocks, resulting in a zig-zag effect. If you choose a border and background print that resembles a skyscape the darker strips will appear to float on a light background. To make this quilt all you have to do is sew together three strips of blue fabric and rotary cut into blocks. This is one of the simplest patterns to strip piece, but the results are, as you can see, quite dramatic. This little quilt, which can either be made into a wall hanging or used by the special little boy in your life, is so easy and quick you won't believe how quickly you'll finish it!

FABRIC QUANTITIES AND CUTTING INSTRUCTIONS

1 ◆ LIGHT BLUE PRINT: 160 cm (1 ¾ yd)

Cut four 6.5 cm (2 ½ in) strips the width of the fabric.

Cut four border panels 16.5 x 91.5 cm (6 ½ x 36 in) strips the width of the fabric.

2 ◆ MEDIUM BLUE PRINT: 35 cm (⅜ yd)

Cut four 6.5 cm (2 ½) strips strips the width of the fabric.

3 ◆ DARK BLUE PRINT: 35 cm (⅜ yd)

Cut four 6.5 cm (2 ½ in) strips strips the width of the fabric.

4 ◆ BACKING:

Cut one backing: 100 x 130 cm (40 x 52 in) from fabric 1 above.

5 ◆ HANGING SLEEVE: 22.5 x 120 cm (8 x 48 in)

See page 36 for assembly instructions.

◆ BATTING: 100 x 130 cm (40 x 52 in)

Key to fabrics

1

2

3

PIECING INSTRUCTIONS

1 Sew one strip of fabrics 1, 2 and 3 together to make a combined strip **(fig 1).** Make four combined strips. Press all seams in one direction. Cut each combined strip into six 16.5 cm (6 ½ in) blocks **(fig 2)** to make 24 blocks (there will be a small piece left over).

fig 1

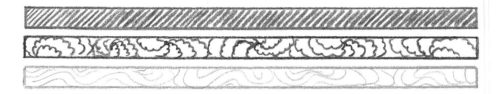

fig 2

ASSEMBLY INSTRUCTIONS:

1 Sew the four blocks together to form a row with the blocks alternating between horizontal and vertical strips **(fig 3).** Make six rows.

fig 3

2 Sew the rows together, with rows alternating between horizontal and vertical strips **(fig 4).**

fig 4

3 Add the borders to the six-block edge first. Sew on the last two borders, as shown in the assembly diagram opposite.

4 Press the quilt top, assemble the sandwich of quilt, batting and backing and then pin and baste. Quilt the top using quilting-in-the-ditch stitch along each of the rails.

5 Trim the batting even with the quilt top. Trim the backing to 1.5 cm (½ in) larger than the batting and top. Self-bind the quilt with the backing fabric. Add a hanging sleeve, if required.

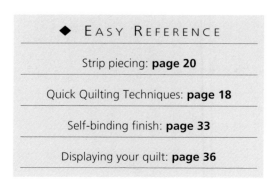

◆ EASY REFERENCE

Strip piecing: **page 20**

Quick Quilting Techniques: **page 18**

Self-binding finish: **page 33**

Displaying your quilt: **page 36**

Assembly of the quilt

SEMINOLE PHOTO ALBUM COVER

◆ *Size: 33 x 27 cm (12 x 10½ in)*

Seminole piecing was invented by the Seminole Indians in Florida as a quick way to trim skirts with bands of fabric. There are many Seminole patterns but this one creates a chevron effect. Using a rotary cutter greatly speeds up this process. This album cover has an A4 folder as a base and is made to look luxurious with a rich touch of gold silk among the dark fabrics. You could consider other colour possibilities, such as white or off-white fabrics for a bride's book, bright primary colours for a cute baby book or wild prints for a teenager's scrapbook.

FABRIC QUANTITIES AND CUTTING INSTRUCTIONS

1 ◆ BLACK AND ORANGE PAISLEY: 25 cm (¼ yd)
Cut two strips 11.5 cm (4 ½) the width of the fabric, and then cut in half.

2 ◆ ORANGE AND BLACK PRINT: 65 cm (1 yd)
Cut two strips 6.5 cm (2 ½) the width of the fabric and then cut in half. Cut two flaps 21.5 cm x 34 cm (8 ½ x 13 ½ in). Cut two backings 35 x 60 cm (14 x 24 in).

3 ◆ GOLD SILK: 65 cm (⅝ yd)
Cut one strip 4 cm (1 ½ in) the width of the fabric and then cut in half. Cut one rectangle 60 x 35 cm (24 x 15 in) to line inside cover of album.

◆ **BATTING:** 35 x 60 cm (14 x 24 in)

ADDITIONAL MATERIALS

◆ **THREAD:** Gold rayon machine embroidery thread.
◆ **COVER BASE:** One A4 folder, with removable ring holder.

Fabric key

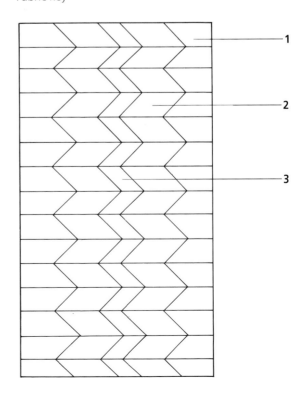

PIECING INSTRUCTIONS

1 Make two sets of strips in stepladder fashion from the fabrics in the following order: Fabrics 1-2-3-2-1. Make sure they are offset in opposite directions **(fig 1)** at an approximate 45° angle. Press the seams all in one direction on one set and in the other direction on the other set.

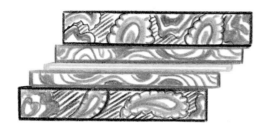

fig 1

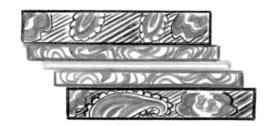

fig 2

2 Cut one strip into 5.5 cm (2 in) strips at a 45° angle to make 15 strips. Cut the second strip on a 45° angle in the opposite direction (to make fifteen 5.5 cm (2 in) strips **(fig 2).**

fig 3

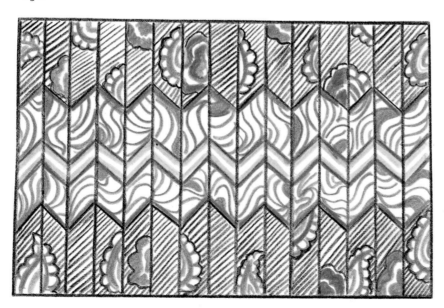

3 Sew the strips together in mirror-image pairs. Join all the strips together vertically and trim the points **(fig 3).** This creates a chevron effect.

4 Assemble the pieced top and the batting, then quilt along the chevrons with gold rayon machine embroidery thread using the quilting-in-the-ditch technique. Trim to measure 21.5 x 57.5 cm (13 ½ x 23 in).

ASSEMBLING THE FOLDER

1 Hem one end of each flap of fabric 2. With right sides together, baste the raw ends of the flaps to each end of the quilted piece.

2 Place the backing, right side down, on top of the right side of the quilted piece **(fig 1)**.

3 Pin and baste. Make sure the flaps are turned onto the backing side of the album cover. Sew round the edges, leaving an opening of approximately 10 cm (4 in). Turn it right side out and slip stitch the opening closed.

4 Cover the inside of the folder with silk, turning over the edges and gluing securely to the front of the folder.

5 Screw on the ring holder and slip the cover onto the folder **(fig 2)**.

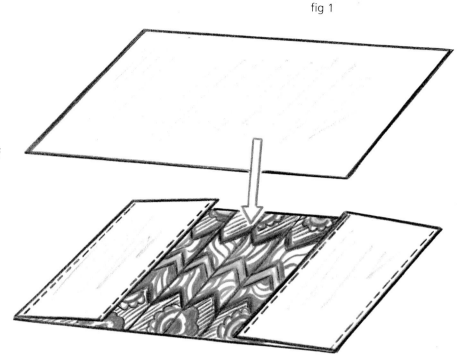

fig 1

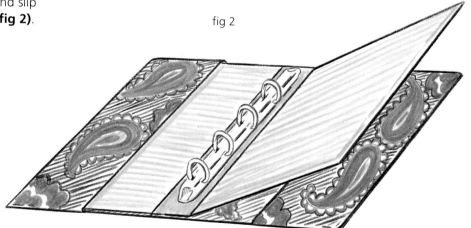

fig 2

◆ EASY REFERENCE

Strip pieced chevrons: **page 21**

Quick Quilting Techniques: **page 30**

SUNSHINE AND SHADOWS QUILT

◆ *Size: 175 x 225 cm (70 x 90 in)*

The Amish people of Lancaster County in Pennsylvania have long kept to their traditional values and isolated themselves from outside worldly influences. They scorn the use of modern machinery and still drive around in horse-and-buggies. The Amish quilters are well known for wonderful handsewn quilts in striking colours and this traditional Amish pattern would have been made of solid fabrics throughout, as their religious beliefs led them to think that prints were frivolous.

Nevertheless, you can't get more frivolous than these two prints: one with multi-coloured stars, the other with multi-coloured animals.

The colour scheme is still Amish, with intense colours against a dark background. I have also used the bright solid colours so favoured by the Amish in the pieced portion of the block. The piecing is speeded up by cutting the triangles from a strip pieced unit. This is a quilt that will definitely bring sweet dreams!

FABRIC QUANTITIES AND CUTTING INSTRUCTIONS

1 ◆ MULTI-COLOURED STARS PRINT: 1.75 x 110 cm (1 ¾ x 44 in)
Cut eighteen squares 27.5 cm (10 ⅞ in). Cut across one diagonal to form 36 triangles. (there will be one triangle left over which you won't need).

2 ◆ MULTI-COLOURED ANIMAL PRINT: 2.75 m (3 yds)
Cut two borders 100 x 26.5 cm (80 x 10 ½ in).
Cut two borders 250 x 26.5 m (100 x 10 ½ in).

3 ◆ NINE SOLID-COLOURED FABRICS: 35 cm (⅜ yd) each
Cut five 6.5 cm (1 ⅞ in) strips of each of the nine solid fabrics.

4 ◆ BACKING: 185 x 235 m (74 x 94 in)

◆ **BATTING:** 185 x 235 m (74 x 94 in)

ADDITIONAL MATERIALS

◆ **TEMPLATE PAPER:** 27.5 x 27.5 cm (10 ⅞ x 10 ⅞ in) of template paper for cutting out solid colour templates.

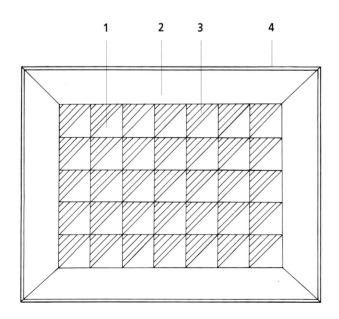

PIECING INSTRUCTIONS

fig 1

1 Prepare the strip pieced triangle pattern by cutting a square of paper 27.5 x 27.5 cm (10 ⅞ x 10 ⅞ in). Cut across on the diagonal. Use one of these triangles as the template for cutting the strip sets of the solid fabrics you will assemble.

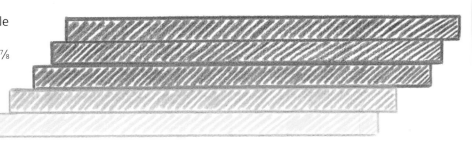

fig 2

2 Sew the strips of solid fabrics together in sets of five, offsetting them to form a stepladder **(fig 1)**. Press all the seams in one direction. From each set of strips cut four triangles, using the paper pattern **(fig 2)**.

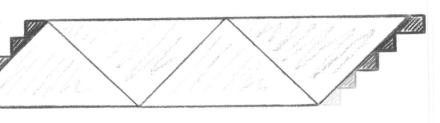

fig 3

3 Sew one pieced triangle unit to one triangle of fabric 1, **(fig 3)**, making 35 blocks.

4 Sew these blocks together in rows of five **(fig 4)**, then sew the rows together.

5 Sew the borders on to all four sides of the quilt. Start .75 cm (¼ in) from each end of the central panel of pieced blocks, using a .75 cm (¼ in) seam.

6 Mitre the corners of the borders. Sew the seams, open out and trim away excess fabric. Press flat.

fig 4

Quilt assembly

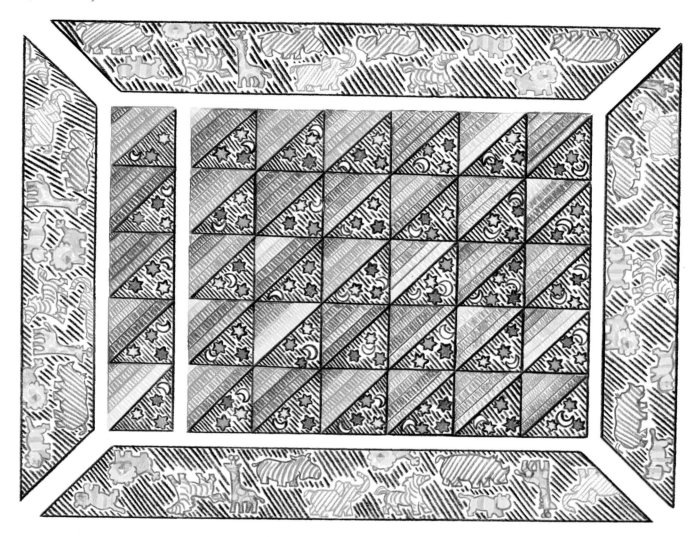

ASSEMBLY INSTRUCTIONS

1 Sandwich the quilt top with the batting and backing fabric. Pin and baste.

2 To quilt, machine diagonally across the quilt top, using the quilting-in-the-ditch technique at the edges of the strips. Machine stitch the borders using a free motion pattern.

3 Trim the batting even with the quilt top. Self-bind the quilt edges with the backing fabric.

◆ EASY REFERENCE

Making and Using Templates: **page 16**

Mitring borders: **page 27**

Quick Quilting Techniques: **page 30**

Self-binding finish: **page 33**

BARGELLO JEWELLERY POUCH

◆ *Size: 35.25 x 25.25 cm (14 x 10 in)*

This little jewellery roll has two zipped compartments and is made from two main colours using the Bargello technique, which imitates the Bargello tapestry stitch. The effect is achieved by using strip piecing and then shifting the pattern to produce a dramatic visual effect with a fluid blend of movement. You will only need one strip of each fabric to make the top and a nifty little trick makes this project extremely easy. Another couple of shortcuts eliminates the need for a lining, as the quilt backing serves this function, and the pouches are added at the same time as the binding.

This handy little gift would be truly appreciated by some lucky friend – or even yourself.

Fabric key

FABRIC QUANTITIES AND CUTTING INSTRUCTIONS

Ten different coloured fabrics, comprising:

1 ◆ PALE MINT PRINT
One 5.25 x 38 cm (2 x 15 in) strip.

2 ◆ PINK AND MINT FLORAL PRINT
One 5.25 x 38 cm (2 x 15 in) strip.

3 ◆ MEDIUM DARK MINT PRINT
One 5.25 x 38 cm (2 x 15 in) strip.

4 ◆ MEDIUM MINT PRINT
One 5.25 x 38 cm (2 x 15 in) strip.

5 ◆ LIGHT MINT PRINT
One 5.25 x 38 cm (2 x 15 in) strip.

6 ◆ MAROON
One 5.25 x 38 cm (2 x 15 in) strip.

7 ◆ PINK AND GREEN CHECK
One 5.25 x 38 cm (2 x 15 in) strip.

8 ◆ PINK PRINT
One 5.25 x 38 cm (2 x 15 in) strip.

9 ◆ PINK, GREEN AND GOLD PRINT
One 5.25 x 38 cm (2 x 15 in) strip.
Four pieces 30 x 21.5 cm (12 x 4 ½ in) for zipped compartments.

10 ◆ DARK GREEN
Two 6 cm (2 ½ in) strips for binding.

11 ◆ BACKING FABRIC: 36 x 48 cm (12 x 16 in)

◆ **BATTING:** 35 x 45 cm (12 x 16 in).

ADDITIONAL MATERIALS
◆ **Zips:** Two 25 cm (10 in) zips.
◆ **Satin bow:** One length pink satin ribbon.

PIECING INSTRUCTIONS

1 Sew the first nine strips of fabric together **(fig 1)**. Sew the first and last strips together to form a tube **(fig 2)**.

fig 1

fig 2

2 From the joined tube cut strips of the following **(fig 3)**:
Two 7.5 cm (2 ½ in) strips (A strips).
Two 5.5 cm (2 in) strips (B strips).
Two 4 cm (1 ½ in) strips (C strips).
One 2.75 cm (1 in) strips (D strip).

There will be a little left over after cutting the strips. This gives you some leeway for error and for cutting a 90° angle to start.

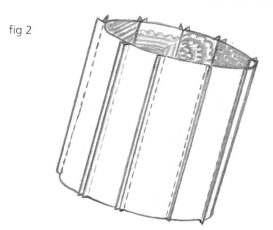

fig 3

3 Pull out the seam line threads between the following fabrics to make different patterns **(fig 4)**:

fig 4

Strip A: pull the thread between fabrics 9 and 1.
Strip B: pull the thread between fabrics 1 and 2.
Strip C: pull the thread between fabrics 2 and 3.
Strip D: pull the thread between fabrics 3 and 4.

4 Sew the strips together again in this order: A-B-C-D-C-B-A **(fig 5)**. This joined piece forms the bargello-effect pouch back.

fig 5

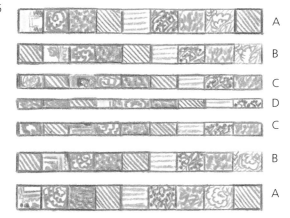

A
B
C
D
C
B
A

ASSEMBLY INSTRUCTIONS

1 On each zip compartment rectangle turn back a .75 cm (¼ in) hem. Baste the hemmed edges of two rectangles to each side of one zip. Sew zip into position using the zipper foot attachment of the sewing machine. Repeat for inserting the other zip in the other rectangle. Sew the zipped compartments together **(fig 1)**.

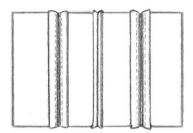

fig 1

2 Assemble the quilt, batting and backing and baste. Quilt the top on the machine to create a random, swirling effect. Trim extra batting and backing even with the top.

3 Place the quilt face down and position the zipped unit face up on top of the backing. Baste into position. Trim edges of pouch even with the quilted top.

Quilt assembly

fig 2

4 Sew along the centre seam of the compartments to separate the two zippered areas.

5 Add the binding around the four edges, mitring the corners **(fig 2)**.

6 Roll up the jewellery holder and attach a pink satin ribbon. You may want to add a snap fastening to make sure your jewellery is secure.

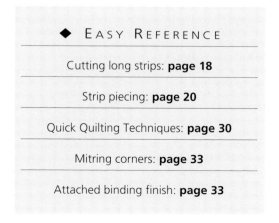

◆ EASY REFERENCE

Cutting long strips: **page 18**

Strip piecing: **page 20**

Quick Quilting Techniques: **page 30**

Mitring corners: **page 33**

Attached binding finish: **page 33**

Lone Star Wall Hanging

◆ *Size: 98 x 98 cm (38 ¾ x 38 ¾ in)*

The Lone Star is a traditional pattern which is sometimes called the Star of Bethlehem. With 288 tiny diamonds, it is a real challenge to make using traditional methods but, by using strip piecing and rotary cutting techniques, this little quilt will be on your wall in a trice! I quilted-in-the-ditch to help anchor the star but also quilted the off-white patches to make them show up. The border print was straight line quilted along the pattern to make its linear quality more prominent.

Fabric key

Fabric Quantities and Cutting Instructions

1 ◆ Dark purple print: 15 cm (⅛ yard)
Cut two 5.25 cm (2 in) strips the width of the fabric.

2 ◆ Light teal print: 25 cm (¼ yd)
Cut four 5.25 cm (2 in) strips the width of the fabric.

3 ◆ Light purple print: 35 cm (⅜ yd)
Cut six 5.25 cm (2 in) strips the width of the fabric.

4 ◆ Dark teal print: 35 cm (⅜ yd)
Cut eight 5.25 cm (2 in) strips the width of the fabric.

5 ◆ Teal and purple print: 50 cm (½ yd)
Cut ten 5.25 cm (2 in) strips the width of the fabric.

6 ◆ Pale teal print: 35 cm (⅜ yd)
Cut six 5.25 cm (2 in) strips the width of the fabric.

7 ◆ Off-white background fabric: 70 cm (¾ yd)
Cut four 24 cm (9 ½ in) squares.
Cut one 35.5 cm (14 in) square. Cut across both diagonals to make four triangles.

8 ◆ Border Print: 115 cm (1 ¼ yard)
Cut four 11.5 cm (4 ½ in) panels the width of the fabric.

9 ◆ Backing: One 105 x 105 cm (42 x 42 in) square

◆ **Batting:** 105 x 105 cm (42 x 42 in)

◆ **Hanging sleeve:** 20 x 98 cm (8 x 38 in)

PIECING INSTRUCTIONS

1 Sew one strip of each of fabrics 1 – 6 together to make one set in the order given for A below. As you sew the strips together, stagger them in stepladder fashion at an approximate 45° angle. **(fig 1):**

Set A: Fabrics 1-2-3-4-5-6. Press seams upwards.

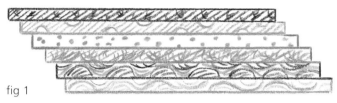

fig 1

2 Repeat this five more times, sewing the six fabrics together in different orders, for sets B – F, as follows:
Set B: Fabrics 2-3-4-5-6-5. Press seams downwards.
Set C: Fabrics 3-4-5-6-5-4. Press seams upwards.
Set D: Fabrics 4-5-6-5-4-3. Press seams downwards.
Set E: Fabrics 5-6-5-4-3-2. Press seams upwards.
Set F: Fabrics 6-5-4-3-2-1. Press seams downwards.
(fig 2).

3 Cut six strips 5.25 cm (2 in) wide from the joined sets at a 45° angle). Check and readjust by trimming the leading edge, if necessary.

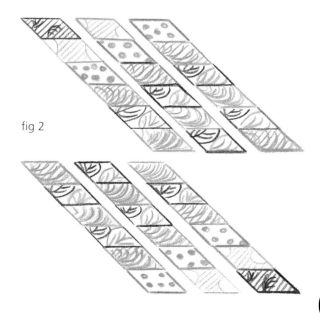

fig 2

4 Make eight pieced diamond units by sewing one strip of each set together in the following order: Set A-B-C-D-E-F **(fig 3).**

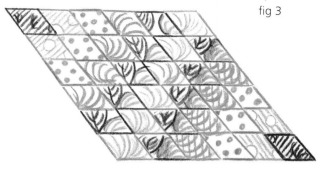

fig 3

5 Sew the diamond units together in pairs. Sew the pairs together to make two half stars **(fig 4).** Open the seams and press flat. Join the two half stars together. Press the seams to one side. Trim points if necessary to reduce bulk. Set in and sew the side triangles and corner squares of fabric 7.

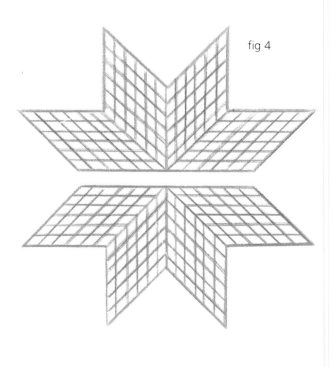

fig 4

6 Sew the four border panels to the top. Mitre the corner of the border panel. Press with an iron.

Quilt assembly

Assembly Instructions

1 Layer the quilt top, batting and backing and baste.

2 Quilt diagonally from left to right across the centre star using the quilting-in-the-ditch method. Quilt again, from right to left. This outlines each of the diamonds comprising the centre star. Quilt the off-white inset triangles and squares with semi-circles. I used straight line quilting along the pattern in the border.

3 Trim the batting even with quilt top. Trim backing to 1.5 cm (½ in) wider than top and batting. Self-bind the edges with the backing fabric, mitring the corners.

4 Make a hanging sleeve.

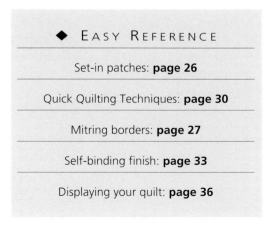

◆ Easy Reference

Set-in patches: **page 26**

Quick Quilting Techniques: **page 30**

Mitring borders: **page 27**

Self-binding finish: **page 33**

Displaying your quilt: **page 36**

REINDEER QUILT

◆ *Quilt size: 170 x 170 cm (68 x 68 in)*

This quilt was inspired by a set of cookie cutters I bought in Denmark, the land where the reindeer flourish. I love this folk art quilt because it so reminds me of the cold, snowy evenings we had when I was living there. It also brings back happy memories of the visits we made to Dyrehaven, the Danish reindeer park where herds of magnificent reindeer run free.

The wonderful prints with gold details give the quilt a rich glow and the multiple borders are arranged medallion-style to frame the centre picture. The blue swirl in the background is painted with silk paints and then machine quilted.

This quilt would look great on a wall, draped over a chair or table, or on the bed. It's sure to be a wintry favourite with all the family.

FABRIC QUANTITIES AND CUTTING INSTRUCTIONS

TRIANGLE TEMPLATES
◆ All the triangles for the quilt pieces are on pages 120-121.

1 ◆ RED REINDEER PRINT: 180 cm (1 ⅞ yd)
Cut sixty R1 triangles. Cut four R2 triangles. Cut four R2 triangles reversed.

2 ◆ GREEN REINDEER PRINT: 180 cm (1 ⅞ yd)
Cut sixty-four R1 triangles.

3 ◆ WHITE PRINT WITH GOLD STARS: 115 cm (1 ¼ yd)
Cut a 106.5 cm (42 ½ in) square.

4 ◆ BLUE PRINT AND GOLD STARS: 50 cm (½ yd)
Cut fifty-six R3 triangles.

5 ◆ RED GOLD & BROWN PRINT: 80 cm (⅞ yd)
Prepare the 5 reindeers using templates (R5 and R6) and freezer paper.

6 ◆ GREEN AND GOLD PRINT: 80 cm (⅞ yd)
Cut out one hundred and eight R3 triangles.
Cut out four R4 triangles.
Cut out four R4 triangles reversed.
Cut out fabric for star and moon templates (R9, R10, R11 and R12).

7 ◆ BLUE PRINT WITH GOLD STARS AND SUN: 60 cm (⅝ yd)
Cut fifty-six R3 triangles.
Cut four 9 cm (3 ½ in) squares.
Cut four 11.5 cm (4 ½ in) squares.
Cut four 16.5 x 16.5 cm (6 ½ x 6 ½ in) squares.

8 ◆ BLUE PRINT WITH GOLD STARS, SUN AND SNOWFLAKES: 160 cm (1 ¾ yd)
Cut four 11.5 x 151.5 cm (4 ½ x 60 ½ in).

Cut eight 6 cm (2 in) strips for binding.

9 ◆ RED PRINT WITH GOLD HOLLY: 25 cm (¼ yd)
Cut out fabric using man template R7.

10 ◆ RED PRINT WITH GOLD DOTS: 25 cm (¼ yd)
Cut out fabric using woman template R8.

11 ◆ BACKING FABRIC: 180 x 180 cm (72 x 72 in)

◆ **BATTING:** 180 x 180 cm (72 x 72 in)

ADDITIONAL MATERIALS
◆ **THREAD:** Colourless monofilament nylon thread. White cotton thread.
◆ **FREEZER PAPER**
◆ **SILK PAINT**
◆ **PAINTBRUSH**

TEMPLATES

Using the templates on page 118-119, cut them out from freezer paper, allowing a .75 cm (¼ in) seam allowance, and apply them to the muslin foundations, as follows:

◆ One of reindeer template R5 and another one, reversed.

◆ Two of reindeer template R6 and one more, reversed.
◆ Two of man template R7.
◆ Two of woman template R8.
◆ Three of star template R9.
◆ Three of star template R10.
◆ Three of star template R11.
◆ One of moon template R12.

PAINTING THE CENTRAL PANEL

1 Dilute a small amount of the turquoise silk paint with water to make a light wash.

2 Use a paintbrush to paint a swirl of blue on to fabric 3. If you don't like the effect, wash out while still wet and start again. Let it dry. If you like the effect, set with your iron according to the directions for the paint you are using.

PIECING INSTRUCTIONS

1 Set the machine to blindstitch and thread the needle with monofilament nylon thread, but use white cotton thread in the bobbin. Set the stitch length very low and adjust the width of the stitch so that the 'V' barely catches the edge of the appliquéd shapes.

2 Pin the shapes to the square of fabric 3. Stitch into place. Trim away the fabric beneath the applied shapes. Dampen the freezer paper and gently tug to remove from the templates.

3 Piece the inner border using fabric 6 R3 green triangles with fabric 4 and 7 R3 blue triangles. Sew four rows with 28 blue and 27 green triangles. Finish the four rows with one R4 triangle of green at each end.

4 Sew a square of fabric 7 to each end of two strips. **(fig 1).**

fig 1

Fabric key

1 2 9 3 4 5 6 10 7 8

5 Piece the middle border sections by sewing the red R1 triangles to the green R1 triangles. Sew four rows with 16 green triangles and 15 red triangles. Finish all 4 rows with an R2 triangle of red at each end. Sew a square of fabric 7 to each end of two strips **(fig 2).**

fig 2

6 Piece the outer border sections by sewing a square of fabric 7 to the ends of two of the unpieced strips of fabric 8.

7 Place a pin at the exact midpoint of each border strip and at the exact midpoint of the edges of the large white square with appliquéd figures.

8 Sew on the first border by matching the centre pins. Sew on the middle border by matching the centre pins. Sew on the last border by matching the centre pins. Sew with a .75 cm (¼ in) seam.

Quilt assembly

ASSEMBLY INSTRUCTIONS

1 Sandwich the quilt top with the batting and backing fabric. Pin and baste.

2 With monofilament nylon thread in the needle and white cotton thread in the bobbin, quilt the top. I've quilted around the figures, stars and reindeers and then swirled in a free-motion fashion all around the borders and the centre. I also free-motion quilted along the blue paint swirls using turquoise machine embroidery thread. Bind the quilt edge with the strips of fabric 8.

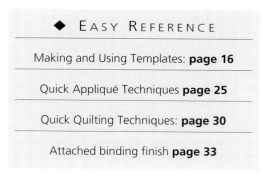

◆ EASY REFERENCE

Making and Using Templates: **page 16**

Quick Appliqué Techniques **page 25**

Quick Quilting Techniques: **page 30**

Attached binding finish **page 33**

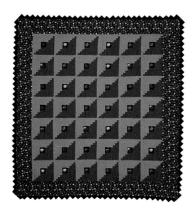

GRANNY SMITH'S LOG CABIN QUILT

◆ *Quilt size 110 x 237.5 cm (84 x 94½ in) (excluding prairie point borders)*

This traditional pattern has been a favourite of quilters since the 1800s. Usually it starts with a red centre to symbolise the hearth but this updated version features an apple in the centre of each cabin. As the apple is a symbol of both the hearth and knowledge I think it works very well on this quilt, both symbolically and artistically. Although Granny Smith apples are my favourite, this quilt features many different apples. The lovely dark colours really set off the apples and make a very dramatic quilt, with the prairie points providing a stunning finishing touch.

Fabric key

FABRIC QUANTITIES AND CUTTING INSTRUCTIONS

1 ◆ APPLE PRINT: 250 cm (2 ⅜ yd)
Cut two strips 185.25 x 27.75 cm (74 x 11 in).
Cut two strips 209 x 27.75 cm (83 ½ x 11 in).

2 ◆ GREEN SOLID: 2.75 m (3 yds)
Cut seventy 4 cm (1 ½ in) strips the width of the fabric.

3 ◆ CRANBERRY SOLID: 2.75 m (2 ¾ yd)
Cut sixty 4 cm (1 ½ in) wide strips the width of the fabric.

4 ◆ LARGE SCALE APPLE PRINT: 75 cm (¾ yd)
Cut forty-two 7.75 cm (3 in) squares with an apple in the centre of each, using a clear plastic template.

5 ◆ BLACK SOLID: 4.5 m (5 yds)
Cut four strips 210 x 27.5 cm (84 x 11 in).
Cut four strips 236.25 x 27.75 cm (94 ½ x 11 in).

6 ◆ FOUNDATIONS (MUSLIN): 3.5 m (3½ yds)
Cut forty-two 27.75 (11 in) squares.

7 ◆ BACKING: 220 x 245 cm (88 x 99 in)

◆ **BATTING:** 220 x 245 cm (88 x 99 in)

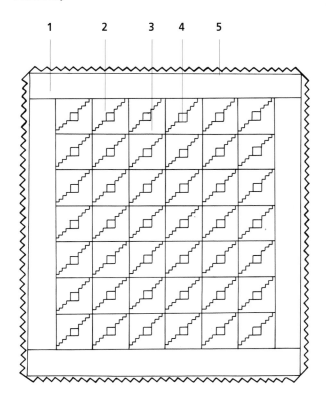

PIECING INSTRUCTIONS

1 Sew an apple square onto the middle of a muslin foundation square. Sew strips around the apple centre in a log cabin pattern. Do this in a sequence of Fabric 2 followed by fabric 3, until you have four concentric rows of each. Press each strip open as it is sewn. Trim. Make forty-two blocks in this way.

2 Assemble the blocks as shown in the assembly diagram. Attach the borders.

ASSEMBLY INSTRUCTIONS

1 Sandwich the quilt top with the batting and backing fabric. Pin and baste.

2 I quilted each block with a continuous spiral line. Then I had fun with my programmable sewing machine and quilted apple shapes all along the border **(fig 1)**. I ended each corner with another apple shape **(fig 2)**.

3 Trim the batting even with the top. Trim the backing, allowing a 1.5 cm (½ in) surplus.

4 Make the prairie points using the strips of fabric 5. Cut the strips at intervals of 26.25 cm (10 ½ in) to form squares for the prairie points. Lay the prairie point strips on top of the quilt and sew with a .75 cm (¼ in) seam. Trim back the seam edges to 1.5 cm (½ in). Turn the points out.

5 Cover the raw edges with the backing by turning under a seam and blindstitching into place.

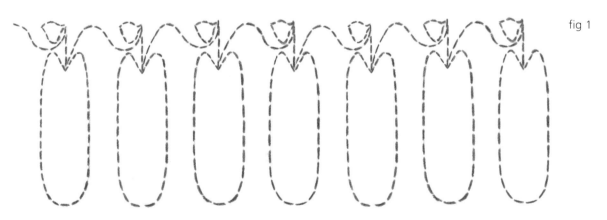

fig 1

fig 2

◆ EASY REFERENCE

Quick Cutting Techniques: **page 18**

Log cabin patchwork: **page 24**

Continuous prairie point borders: **page 34**

Quilt assembly

PINEAPPLE CUSHION

◆ *Quilt size: 30 x 30 cm (12 x 12 in)*

The pineapple pattern is a traditional version of the log cabin design. I have used nine 7.5 cm (3 in) blocks to create a complex pattern. Using the traditional method of separate templates for each trapezoid shape would make the assembly of each block very time-consuming but you can overcome this by piecing the cushion on the machine over paper foundations. If you have trouble positioning the strips before sewing, cut them slightly oversize to make it easier to place the strips. If you prefer this method, all the strips should be cut 3 cm (1 ½ in) wide for ease in positioning. It is very helpful to use a light box when positioning the fabric onto the pattern.

FABRIC QUANTITIES AND CUTTING INSTRUCTIONS

Cut out the fabrics (see fabric key on page 98), as follows:

1 ◆ BLACK AND WHITE PRINT (1): 15 cm (⅛ yd)
Cut one strip 2.5 cm (⅞ in) the width of the fabric.

2 ◆ RED AND BLACK PRINT: 15 cm (⅛ yd)
Cut two strips 2.5 cm (⅞ in) the width of the fabric.

3 ◆ RED AND WHITE PRINT (1): 15 cm (⅛ yd)
Cut two strips 2.5 cm (⅞ in) the width of the fabric.

4 ◆ RED AND WHITE (2): 15 cm (⅛ yd)
Cut three strips 2.5 cm (⅞ in) the width of the fabric.

5 ◆ RED SOLID: 15 cm (⅛ yd)
Cut nine 6.5 cm (2 ½ in) squares.

6 ◆ WHITE AND RED PRINT: 15 cm (⅛ yd)
Cut two strips 2.5 cm (⅞ in) the width of the fabric.

7 ◆ GREY AND BLACK PRINT: 15 cm (⅛ yd)
Cut two strips 2.5 cm (⅞ in) the width of the fabric.

8 ◆ BLACK AND WHITE PRINT (2): 15 cm (⅛ yd)
Cut two strips 2.5 cm (⅞ in) the width of the fabric.

9 ◆ BLACK AND WHITE PRINT (3): 60 cm (⅝ yd)
Cut one strip 2.5 cm (⅞ in) the width of the fabric. Cut two backing squares 50 x 50 cm (20 x 20 in) (one for cushion back and one for layering with batting and quilt top).

10 ◆ BLACK AND WHITE PRINT (4): 15 cm (⅛ yd)
Cut one strip 2.5 cm (⅞ in) the width of the fabric.

11 ◆ BLACK AND WHITE PRINT (5): 15 cm (⅛ yd)
Cut one strip 2.5 cm (⅞ in) the width of the fabric.

12 ◆ SOLID BLACK: 20 cm (¼ yd)
Cut three 4 cm (2 in) strips the width of the fabric.

13 ◆ GREY AND BLACK PRINT: 15 cm (⅛ yd)
Cut two strips 2.5 cm (⅞ in) the width of the fabric.

14 ◆ WHITE SOLID: 25 cm (¼ yd)
Cut three strips 2.5 cm (⅞ in) the width of the fabric. Cut one strip 4 cm (1 ½ in) the width of the fabric.

15 ◆ CORDING COVER: 130 cm (1 ½ yd)
Cut 135 cm (54 in) of bias strips 6 cm (2 in) wide to cover piping cord.

◆ **BATTING:** 25 cm (¼ yd)
Cut one square 50 x 50 cm (20 x 20 in).

ADDITIONAL MATERIALS

◆ **TRACING PAPER:** For making foundations.
◆ **PIPING CORD:** 135 cm (54 in).
◆ **CUSHION PAD:** 30 cm (12 in) square.

PIECING INSTRUCTIONS

Fabric key: Position your choice of fabrics to recreate the different tonal values of the three types of block below, following the photograph and illustrations.

This is a variation of the log cabin method. Prepare nine paper pineapple patterns by tracing the template PC1 (imperial) on page 123 or PC1(M) (metric) on page 124. Follow the piecing diagrams to place the strips. Make one centre block. Make four corner blocks and make four of Block X.

Centre block   Corner block

Block X

MAKING PINEAPPLE BLOCKS
Make nine pineapple blocks as follows:

1 Place the paper pattern face down on the light box and centre the red square in the middle. Position the first fabric strip with the right side facing down in one corner of the square at a 45° angle **(fig 1)**. Pin in place.

fig 1

2 Set the machine stitch length on the machine to slightly lower than normal.

3 Flip the pattern over and sew on the line between the centre square and patch 1 **(fig 2)**. Trim to .75 cm (¼ in) from the seam and press the seam open.

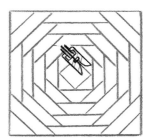

fig 2

4 Position the second strip with the right side facing down in the next corner of the square at a 45° angle. Pin in place. Flip the pattern over and sew on the line between the centre square and patch 2. Trim to .75 cm (¼ in) from the seam and press the seam open **(fig 3)**. Repeat twice to finish this round.

fig 3

Assembly of the cushion

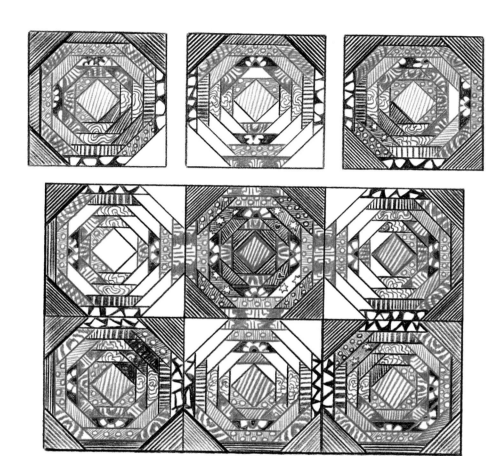

5 Continue positioning, sewing, trimming and pressing the strips. Work in a circular fashion until the block is complete.

6 Sew three blocks into rows and then sew the three rows together to complete the top. Remove the tracing paper patterns.

ASSEMBLY INSTRUCTIONS

1 Place the pineapple patchwork face up on a flat surface. Pin the pre-covered cording around the four sides of the patchwork, neatly tucking in the two ends of the cording. Trim the patchwork to .75 cm (¼ in) from the edge of the cording. Baste the cording into place.

2 Place the backing fabric face down on top of the piping. Sew with a .75 cm (¼ in) seam. Leave a 15 cm (6 in) gap along one edge to turn. Clip the corners to reduce the bulk. Turn out the cushion to the right side. Press and then insert the cushion pad. Handstitch the opening closed.

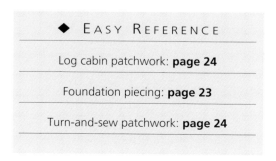

◆ EASY REFERENCE

Log cabin patchwork: **page 24**

Foundation piecing: **page 23**

Turn-and-sew patchwork: **page 24**

CRAZY QUILTED TABLE RUNNER

◆ *Quilt size: 30 x 120 cm (12 x 48 in)*

You can make this table runner very easily on your machine using the crazy quilting technique. The embroidery embellishments can be sewn by hand, as shown, or you could make use of some of the fancy stitches on your machine. You can either use many different stitches and thread colours or just use one stitch and one colour on all the seams. This table runner will look great on the dining table for special occasions.

ASSEMBLY INSTRUCTIONS

1 Make the four crazy blocks, including the two with pointed ends, as follows :

Cut a four to six-sided fabric scrap and place in the centre of one of the foundations with the right side facing up. Place a second scrap facing down and aligned with one side of the first scrap. Sew a .75 cm (¼ in) seam. Trim any excess fabric to .75 cm (¼ in) of the seam. Press the seam open **(fig 1).**

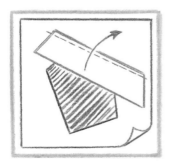

fig 1

2 Place a third scrap facing down and align with second edge of the centre square. The scrap must extend past the edges of both of the first two patches.

FABRIC QUANTITIES AND CUTTING INSTRUCTIONS

1 ◆ 2–3 YARDS OF SCRAPS OF FANCY FABRICS

2 ◆ ½ YD COTTON MUSLIN
Cut four 31.5 cm (12 ½ in) squares of cotton muslin to use for the foundations. Cut the one end of two foundations into an even point.

3 ◆ BACKING: 31.5 x 121.5 cm (12 ½ x 48 ½ in)

ADDITIONAL MATERIALS

◆ **THREAD:** Gold embroidery thread.
◆ **FRINGE:** 1 metre (3 yds) gold fringe.

3 Continue working in a circular fashion until all the block is covered by fabric scraps. Trim the fabric which extends past the .75 cm (¼ in) seam allowance of the block. Make four blocks in this way.

4 Sew the four blocks together in a row with the two pointed blocks on each end pointing outwards.

◆ EASY REFERENCE

Crazy patchwork: **page 23**

Assembly diagram

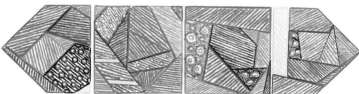

EMBROIDERY AND ASSEMBLY INSTRUCTIONS

1 Using the gold embroidery thread and an embroidery needle, sew along the scraps where they join, using a variety of stitches. For example, you could use a combination of traditional crazy patchwork stitches such as blanket stitch, herringbone stitch, feather stitch and Cretan stitch, as I have done.

2 Baste the fringe to the top. To do this, place the backing, right side down, onto the quilt. Placing the beginning of the fringe in the centre (with the fringes inside the two layers of material), baste into position all around the runner. Machine sew all around the edge with a .75 cm (¼ in) seam allowance, leaving 15 cm (6 in) unsewn.

3 Trim the backing and clip the corners. Turn to the right side through the unsewn opening and press. Sew the opening closed by hand.

LEAF CUSHION

◆ *Cushion size: 45 x 45 cm (18 x 18 in)*

This leafy cushion of autumnal colours is pieced on a foundation of paper (later removed) and was made by using various scraps of hand-painted and dyed fabrics.

You could splatter drops of silk paint onto solid colours of fabrics to achieve an interesting effect. You could even use crumpled up pieces of solid fabric dipped in silk paint to achieve an attractive tie-dye effect. Shop-bought prints would also work well – look out for those with leafy autumnal colours and designs.

Using a light box will help enormously when you are positioning the pieces and quilting along the arrows helps to add definition and texture to the cushion. Set the machine stitch length to slightly lower than normal so you can perforate the paper patterns as you sew. This will make removing the paper much easier.

FABRIC QUANTITIES AND CUTTING INSTRUCTIONS

1 ◆ AUTUMNAL COLOURED SCRAPS OF FABRIC
Thirty-six 10 x 22.5 cm (4 x 9 in) scraps for each leaf, cut as follows:
One 9 cm (3 ½ in) square.
Two 4 cm (1 ½ in) squares.
One 4 x 6.5 cm (1 ½ x 2 ½ in) rectangle.
One 4 x 9 cm (1 ½ in x 3 ½ in) rectangle.

◆ BACKING AND CUSHION BACK
Two 50 cm x 50 cm (20 x 20 in) squares of the fabric of your choice.

◆ BATTING
One 50 cm x 50 cm (20 x 20 in) square.

ADDITIONAL MATERIALS
◆ **CUSHION PAD:** One 45 cm (18 in) square cushion pad.

◆ **TYPING PAPER:** Uncoated or other thin paper.

◆ **LIGHT BOX:** For positioning the patterns.

◆ **PERMANENT INK FINE-LINE MARKER PEN**

CUTTING INSTRUCTIONS

1 Prepare 36 paper patterns by tracing the template LC1 (imperial) on page 123 or LC1(M) (metric) on page 124. Draw a scale drawing of the cushion, showing all the colours you are using. Code each area with a number. You will use this to help you correctly piece the small triangles of each block. These triangles must match up with the correct leaf section next to them or the effect will be spoiled.

PIECING INSTRUCTIONS

1 Place the pattern face down on the light box. Place a 9 cm (3 ½ in) square of the leaf fabric (right side facing up) in the corner of the square aligned with the tip of the leaf **(fig 1)**. Using your scale drawing, choose the correct colour of 4 cm (1 ½ in) of fabric and lay it right side down. Align as shown **(fig 2)**. Pin in position.

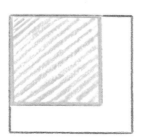 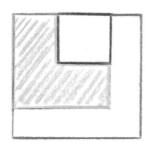

fig 1   fig 2

2 Turn over the pattern and sew on the line between patch 1 and patch 2 **(fig 3)**. Trim .75 cm (¼ in) from the seam. Open the seam flat and press.

fig 3

3 Position the next 4 cm (1 ½ in) square of fabric (refer to the diagram to choose the correct colour) in the large square and pin, as shown in the diagram **(fig 4)**. Turn over the pattern and sew on the line between patch 1 and patch 3 **(fig 5)**. Trim .75 cm (¼ in) from the seam. Open the seam flat and press.

fig 4   fig 5

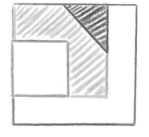 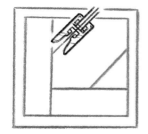

4 Place the 4 x 6.5 cm (1 ½ x 2 ½ in) rectangle of leaf fabric face down on the square and pin in position, as shown in the diagram **(fig 6)**. Turn over and sew on the line between patch 2 and patch 4 **(fig 7)**. Trim, then open the seam flat and press.

 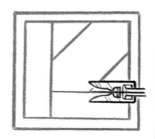

fig 6   fig 7

5 Place the longer rectangle of fabric face down and align with the side and bottom edge of the pieced unit. Pin into position **(fig 8)**. Sew the seam between patch 3 and patch 5 **(fig 9)**. Trim, then open the seam flat and press.

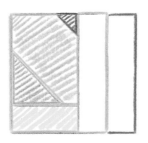 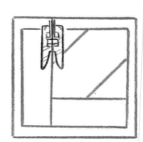

fig 8   fig 9

The finished block

6 Make thirty-six blocks in this way, taking care to piece the colours correctly for the small triangles. Each triangle should match the main colour of the patch next to it.

7 Sew the blocks into rows of six. Sew the rows together. Gently remove the paper foundations.

Quilt
assembly

ASSEMBLY INSTRUCTIONS

1 Press the quilt top and mark the quilting lines with the permanent fine-line marker pen so that they go through the centre of the arrows in a diagonal line.

2 Sandwich the quilt top with the batting and backing fabric. Baste and then machine quilt the lines with a thread that blends with most of your fabrics.

3 Trim the backing and batting so that they are even with the edges of the quilt top. Lay face it up on the table.

2 Place the cushion backing face down on the pieced top and pin into position. Sew with a .75 cm (¼ in) seam, leaving 10 to 15 cm (4 to 6 in) open on one side. Clip the corners to reduce the bulk.

3 Turn the quilt right side out again, press and then insert the cushion pad. Handstitch the opening on the cover closed.

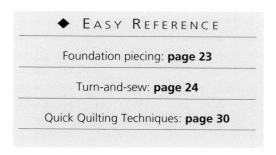

◆ EASY REFERENCE

Foundation piecing: **page 23**

Turn-and-sew: **page 24**

Quick Quilting Techniques: **page 30**

FLYING GEESE BAG

◆ *Quilt size: 37.5 x 50 cm (15 x 20 in)*

This nifty bag has three pouches to hold all your goodies. Choose one printed fabric for the strap, backing and large centre square and two solid colours for the flying geese border.

The flying geese units are quick-cut from squares and are sewn together in assembly line fashion. The patchwork is only a border around a large square of fabric.

After machine quilting, apply the binding to finish off the edges of the square. The bag starts as a large quilted square but, by making two seams and doing some clever folding, the three pouches magically appear as the backing of the quilt becomes the lining of the inner pouches, with all the edges already finished off. Add a strap and you're done!

FABRIC QUANTITIES AND CUTTING INSTRUCTIONS

1 ◆ ORANGE SOLID: 35 cm (⅜ yd)
Cut eight 13.5 cm (5 ¼ in) squares. Cut on both diagonals to make 32 triangles.

2 ◆ TURQUOISE SOLID: 35 cm (½ yd)
Cut ten 13.5 cm (5 ¼ in) squares. Cut on both diagonals to make 40 triangles.

3 ◆ BLACK SOLID: 50 cm (½ yd)
Cut seventy-two 7.5 cm (2 ⅞ in) squares. Cut on one diagonal to make 144 triangles.

4 ◆ ORANGE, BLUE, GOLD, BLACK PRINT: 235 cm (2 ⅜ yd)
Cut one 76.5 cm (32 ½ in) square.

Cut one 110 cm (44 in) square for backing.
Cut one strap 100 x 20 cm (40 x 8 in).
Cut five binding strips 6 cm (2 in) the width of the fabric.

◆ BATTING: 130 x 110 cm (50 x 44 in)
Cut one 110cm (44 in) square.
Cut one 115 cm x 7.5 cm (3 x 44 in) strip for the strap.

ADDITIONAL MATERIALS

◆ **DECORATIVE CLOSURE** (optional).
◆ **TWO LARGE HOOK AND EYE SETS** (optional).

Fabric key

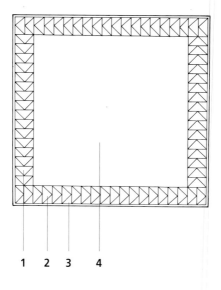

1   2   3   4

PIECING INSTRUCTIONS

1 Sew the long sides of 32 triangles of fabric 3 to one short side of triangles of fabric 1 in assembly line fashion **(fig. 1)**. Sew 32 more triangles of fabric 3 to the other side of the fabric 3 triangles **(fig 2)**. This makes 32 flying geese units. Make 40 flying geese units with fabrics 2 and 3.

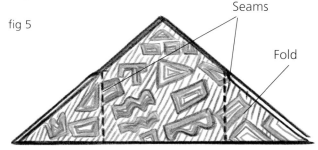

fig 1   fig 2

2 Sew the 18 turquoise units into a row. Make 2 rows. Sew the 18 orange units into a row. Make two rows. **(fig 3)**.

fig 3

3 Sew the flying geese strips to the smaller square of fabric 4 **(fig 4)**.

fig 4

4 Sandwich the quilt top with the batting and backing fabric. Pin and baste.

5 Join the five binding strips together and bind the edges of the quilt.

ASSEMBLY INSTRUCTIONS

1 Place the finished quilt with the top uppermost on a table. Fold the quilt in half diagonally, so that the right sides of the top layer are both together and the backing fabric is outermost. This makes a triangle shape with a long base. Sew a seam one third of the way from the lower right point across the long folded edge. Sew another seam the same distance from the other point **(fig 5)**.

fig 5

Seams

Fold

2 Fold the right hand point in, making the fold along the stitched seam. Do the same for the lefthand side. as shown in **fig 5** above.

3 Separate the two right sides of the fabric of the pouch. Pull the layer over the bottom point, pushing the point up and wrapping the fabric round it. **(fig 6)**. Repeat on the lefthand side.

fig 6

Separate the fold

Fold the fabric back

The assembled bag

fig 2

MAKING AND ATTACHING THE STRAP

1 Position the batting in the centre of the long strap fabric. Fold over a hem on each of the long sides. Fold one hemmed side over the other **(fig 1).** Pin into position. Tuck in the ends of the strap neatly and hem. Machine-sew the length of the centre seam. Also sew .75 cm (¼ in) along the length of the strap on each side.

2 Insert the strap ends into the sides of the centre opening of the bag. Sew into position **(fig 2).** Turn the flaps of the bag down, one on each side. You may wish to attach decorative fastenings to the flaps.

fig 1

◆ EASY REFERENCE

Assembly line piecing: **page 20**

Attached binding finish: **page 33**

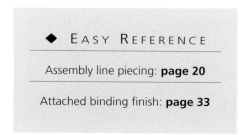

STRING PIECED STAR QUILT

◆ *Quilt size: 185 x 237.5 cm (74 x 95 in) (excluding prairie point border)*

Isn't this a delightful quilt and doesn't it make you want to snuggle up under it? The rich, warm hues of all the different fabrics combine together to make a lovely, harmonious autumn-toned quilt that is dramatically offset by the continuous prairie point border finish. To help blend all the fabrics together I used a tea dye to mellow the material and give them that gentle glow of age. Making this quilt is also a great way to use up scraps of fabric left over from other projects.

The quilt is made by string-piecing the fabrics over paper templates instead of using the more traditional fabric foundations our ancestors would have used.

FABRIC QUANTITIES AND CUTTING INSTRUCTIONS

Use left over scraps from the yardage below to make up some of the fabric diamonds. You will also need lots of other scraps of fabric in complementary colours.

1 ◆ FLORAL PRINT: 2.5 m (2 ½ yds)
Cut two rectangles 11.5 x 219 cm
(4 ½ x 87 ½ in).
Cut two rectangles 11.5 x 219 cm
(4 ½ x 66 ½ in).

2 ◆ RED, GOLD, AND GREEN PAISLEY:
35 cm (⅜ yd)
Cut twenty 9 cm (3 ½ in) squares.
Cut four 11.5 cm (4 ½ in) squares.

3 ◆ RED BRICK FABRIC: 1.65 m (1 ⅝ yds)
Cut thirty-one 9 x 46.5 cm (3 ½ x 18 ½ in)
sash strips.

4 ◆ RED STAR PRINT: 2.75 m (2 ¾ yds)
Cut two 20.5 x 237.5 cm (10 ½ x 95 in).
Cut two 26.5 x 187.5 cm (10 ½ x 75 in).

5 ◆ BLUE STAR FABRIC: 2. 75 m (2 ¾ yds)
Cut two 34.5 x 237.5 cm (10 ½ x 95 in).
Cut two 26.5 x 187.5 cm (10 ½ x 75 in).

6 ◆ CREAM SWIRL PRINT: 2.75 m (2 ¾ yds)
Cut forty-eight 14.75 cm (5 ¾ in). Cut
twelve 22 cm (8 ¾ in) squares. Cut on both
diagonals to make 192 triangles.

7 ◆ BACKING: 1.95 x 2.48 m (78 x 99 in)

◆ BATTING: 1.95 x 2.48 m (78 x 99 in)
Cut to 247.5 x 195 cm (99 x 78 in).

ADDITIONAL MATERIAL

◆ **TYPING PAPER:** for making templates.

Fabric key

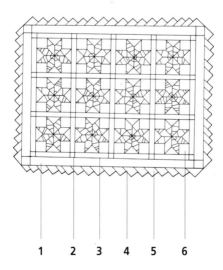

1   2   3   4   5   6

PIECING INSTRUCTIONS

1 Cut 96 paper foundations of the diamond template SP1 (page 122). Then, lay a scrap of fabric, right side up, on one end of a diamond. Lay another scrap, right side down, on top of the first scrap **(fig 1)**.

fig 1

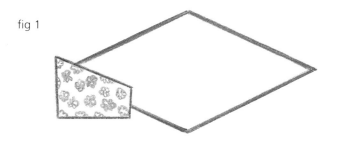

2 Lower the stitch length on your machine to help perforate the paper as you sew. Sew .75 cm (¼ in) from the inner edge, through the fabrics and the paper template. Press open. Place the next scrap **(fig 2).** Sew the seam. Press. Continue until the paper pattern is covered. Make sure that all of the strips extend past the edge of the template. Cut the fabrics back to the edge of the pattern. Make 96 diamonds in this way.

fig 2

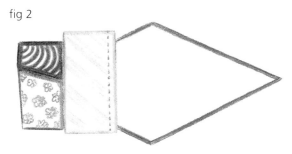

3 Remove the papers and sew the diamonds together in pairs. Sew the pairs together to form half a star **(fig 3)**. Press seam allowances all in one direction. Sew the halves together and press last seam to one side.

fig 3

4 Following the quilt assembly diagram, set in the squares and triangles of fabric 6.

5 Sew the sashes of fabric 3 and the pieced star blocks together in a row. Sew the sashes and squares of fabric 2 into rows. Sew the horizontal sash strips to the rows. Sew the rows together, following the quilt assembly diagram.

6 Attach the vertical borders of fabric 1. Sew the corner squares to the horizontal borders of fabric 2. Attach the horizontal borders.

ASSEMBLY INSTRUCTIONS

1 Press the quilt top. Layer the quilt sandwich with the quilt top, batting and backing. Pin and baste.

2 Stipple quilt by machine in the cream set-in squares and triangles.

3 Make the prairie points using the strips of fabrics 2 and 4. Cut to .75 cm (¼ in) of the seam line every 12.5 cm (5 in).

4 Lay the prairie point strips on top of the quilt and sew with a .75 cm (¼ in) seam. Trim back the seam edges to 1.5 cm (½ in). Turn the points out.

5 Cover the raw edges with the backing by turning under a seam and blindstitching into place.

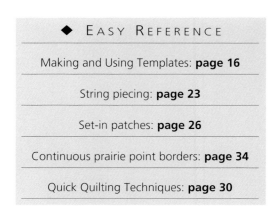

◆ EASY REFERENCE
Making and Using Templates: **page 16**
String piecing: **page 23**
Set-in patches: **page 26**
Continuous prairie point borders: **page 34**
Quick Quilting Techniques: **page 30**

Quilt assembly

TEA DYING

◆ To dye the fabric scraps, brew a strong pot of tea, then soak the fabric in it for at least one hour. Dry and then press the scraps with an iron set on high. Wash the scraps to check for colour fastness.

STRING PIECED WALL HANGING

◆ *Quilt size: 75 x 100 cm (30 x 40 in)*

This striking wall quilt features bold splashes of colour that suggest a sunset over waves. The colours merge and flow – teals and purples blend into magenta, orange and yellow. The various coloured strips are string pieced over papers and then blindstitched together.

Although this looks like a difficult quilt to make, the combination of quick and easy techniques used makes piecing these curves so easy and the grid system will also help you.

BLENDING FABRIC COLOURS

◆ Try to have a range of colours available which will blend from one colour tone to the next. Good fabrics to use as blender scraps are those which have several of the colours in the fabric. Use a scrap with magenta, red-violet and violet to blend from magenta to violet. To bridge the gap between yellow and orange, use a scrap having both colours. Include both pale tints and dark shades of the colours.

FABRIC QUANTITIES AND CUTTING INSTRUCTIONS

1 ◆ 10 FABRIC SCRAPS:
Use a variety in yellow, orange, magenta, violet, purple and teal. Cut them to varying widths ranging from 5–20 cm (2–8 in) and long enough to cover the width of the paper strip you are cutting.

2 ◆ BINDING: 25 cm (¼ yd)
Cut four 6 x 110 cm (2 x 44 in) strips on the straight of grain.

3 ◆ BACKING: 1 metre (1 yd)
Cut to 85 x 115 cm (34 x 44 in).

◆ BATTING: 75 x 100 cm (30 x 40 in)
Cut to 85 x 115 cm (34 x 44 in).

◆ FABRIC FOR HANGING SLEEVE: 20 x 100 cm (8 x 40 in)

ADDITIONAL MATERIAL

◆ **PAPER:** A large sheet 90 cm x 105 cm (32 x 42 in) for the grid.

Use assorted fabric scraps for main design

PIECING INSTRUCTIONS

1 Draw a grid of 25 cm (10 in) squares on the paper to make a pattern 75 x 100 cm (30 x 40 in). Enlarge the SPW1 template (page 123), square by square.

2 Cut out part A of the paper pattern and piece this first. Place paper pattern face up. Position the first strip of fabric face up at one end **(fig 1).**

fig 1

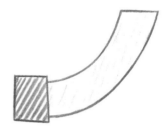

3 Place second piece of fabric, right side down, on top of the first one, matching the edges where you want to sew a seam. Sew a .75 cm (¼ in) seam along the inside edge. Trim the excess fabric and press the seam open **(fig 2)**. Continue sewing and pressing until the strip is covered **(fig 3).**

fig 2

fig 3

4 Cut off part B of the paper pattern and cover in the same way. Continue in this way covering C–G of the paper pattern with the relevant fabrics.

5 On all the strips except the top strip (the sun), turn the top seam allowance over the paper pattern and glue in place. Smooth out all the wrinkles.

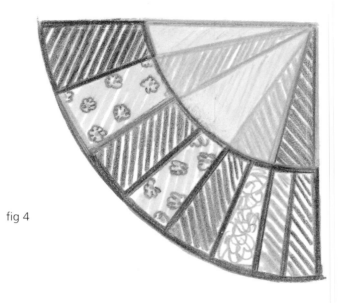

fig 4

6 Place each pattern piece so that it overlaps the loose seam allowances of the previous pattern, with right sides up **(fig 4).**

7 Set your machine to blindstitch. Lower the stitch length until the 'V' closes. Set the stitch width so that the 'V' will catch the edge of the strip underneath. Sew all the parts together in the same way.

8 Remove the papers by dampening to loosen the glue and then tugging gently.

ASSEMBLY INSTRUCTIONS

1 Sandwich the quilt top together with the batting and backing fabric. Pin and baste.

2 Quilt the quilt top using a free motion design. Trim the quilt top and batting and square off the corners. Trim the backing to 1.5 cm (½ in).

3 Join up the binding strips. Press lightly in half and then attach the binding around the edges of the quilt. Blindstitch to the back to finish.

4 Attach a hanging sleeve.

Quilt assembly

◆ EASY REFERENCE

String piecing: **page 23**

Quick Quilting Techniques: **page 30**

Attached binding finish: **page 33**

Displaying your quilt: **page 36**

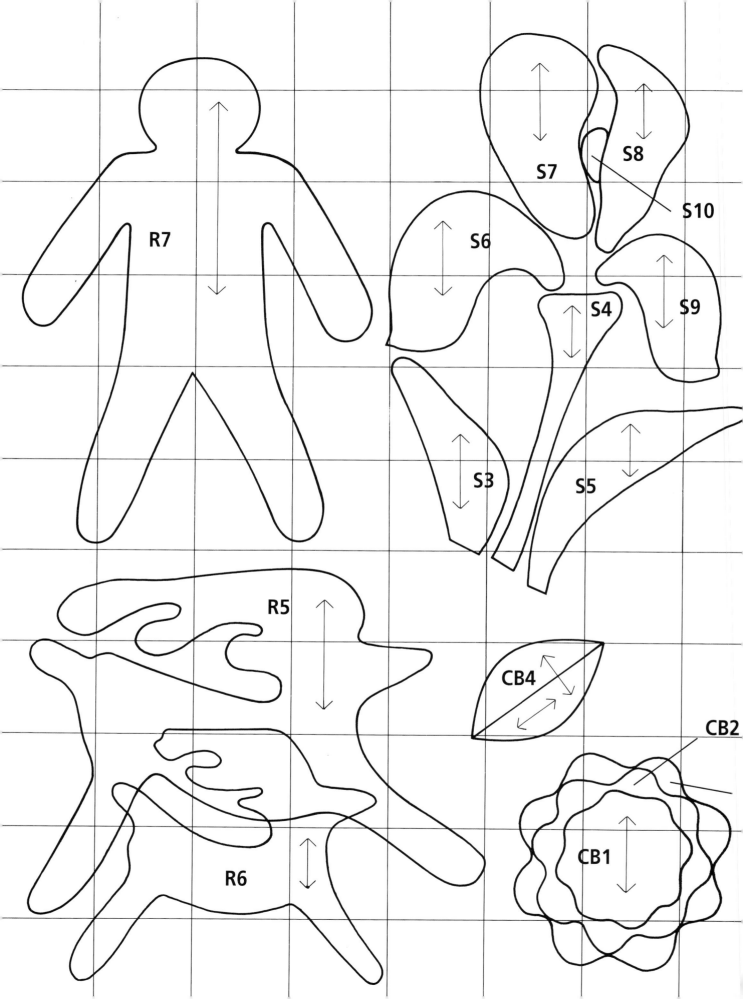

APPLIQUE TEMPLATES

◆ The applique templates here need to be enlarged. To do this, either enlarge them on a photocopier to 200% or use the grid marked on the page. The grid scale is one square equals 10 cm (2 in).

B1

B2

H2 H1
H3

R9

R8

R10

R11

R12

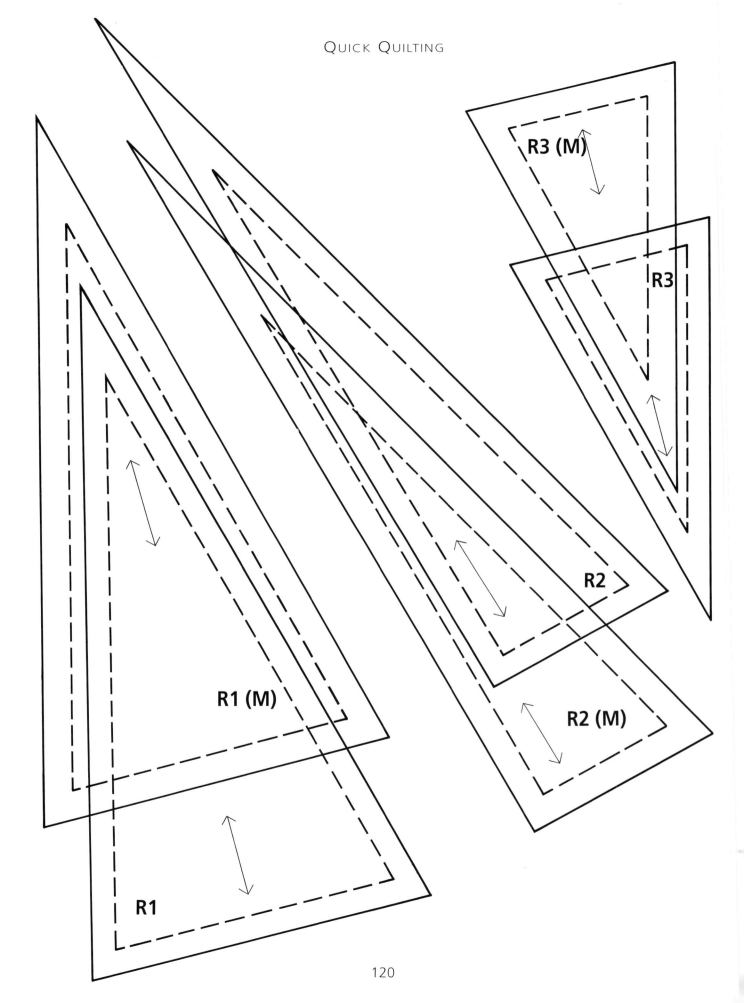

R3 (M)

R3

R2

R1 (M)

R2 (M)

R1

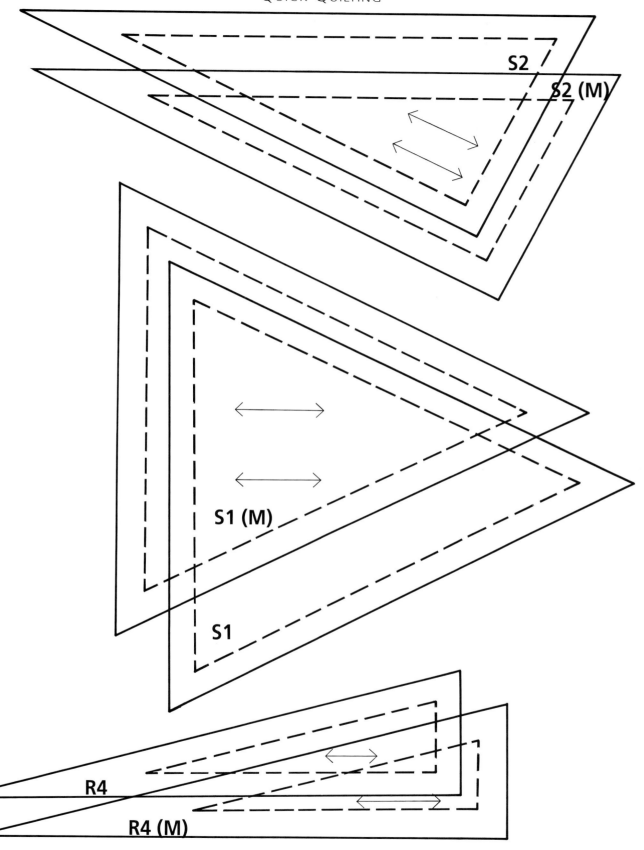

S2

S2 (M)

S1 (M)

S1

R4

R4 (M)

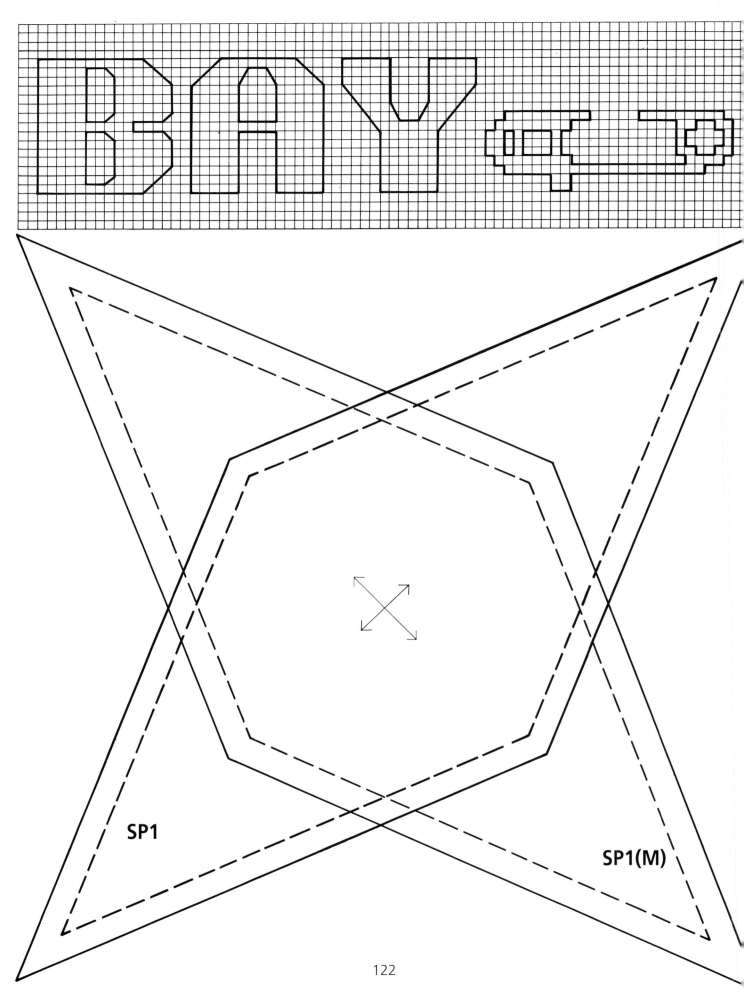

SP1

SP1(M)

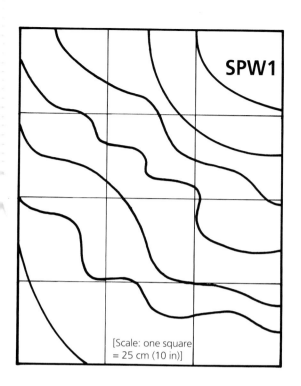

SPW1

[Scale: one square = 25 cm (10 in)]

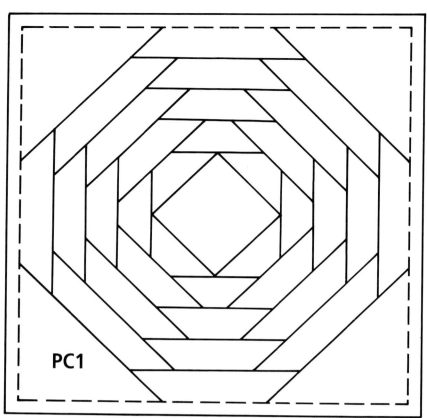

PC1

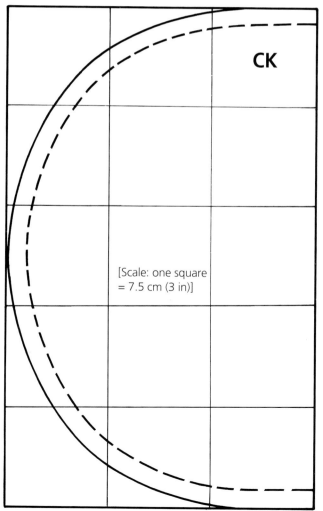

CK

[Scale: one square = 7.5 cm (3 in)]

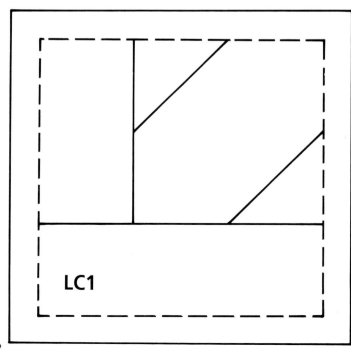

LC1

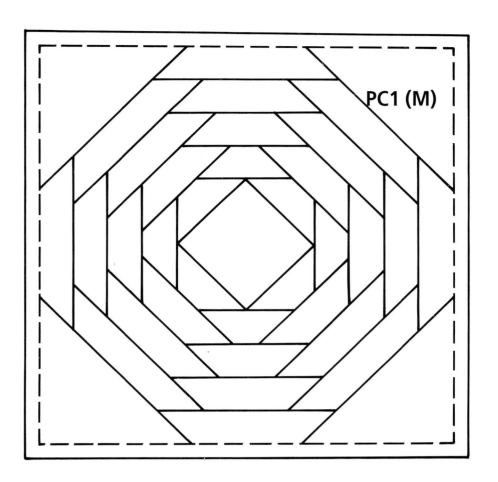

PC1 (M)

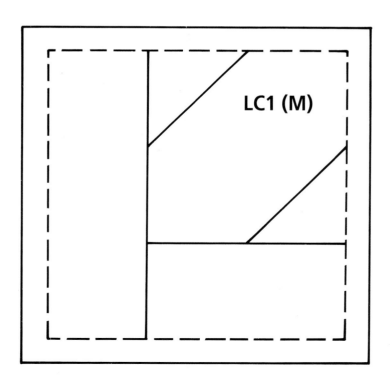

LC1 (M)

ACKNOWLEDGEMENTS

I would like to thank my family and particularly my husband, John, for believing in me and putting up with the mess! I would also like to express my gratitude to Pippa Abrahams for all her support. Thanks, too, to Colleen and Tony Sharkey for all their encouragement during the writing (and ranting) of the book.

I am grateful to Kacy Ritter, Perry Ritter, Colleen Sharkey and Pat Williams for helping to tie the Bunny Quilt and for all their constructive suggestions. I would also like to thank Kay Hendricks, Willy McKinney and Brent Hendricks for all their encouragement.

I really appreciate all the hard work done by Clare Hill, Sue Rawkins and Karen Hemingway for making my book a reality.

QUILTING CONTACTS

QUILTING SOCIETIES, GUILDS AND ORGANISATIONS
Contact them for help and advice.

GREAT BRITAIN
The Quilters Guild
PO Box 66
Dean Cough Business Park
Halifax HX3 5AX

National Patchwork Association
PO Box 300
Hethersett
Norwich
Norfolk NR9 3BD

AUSTRALIA
Queensland Quilters Inc
GPO Box 2841
Brisbane QLD 4001

The Quilters Guild of New South Wales
PO Box 654
Neutral Bay Junction NSW 2089

Quilters Guild of South Australia Inc
PO Box 993
Kent Town SA 5067

Western Australian Quilters Association
PO Box 188
Subiaco WA 6008

Canberra Quilters Inc
PO Box 29
Jamison ACT 2614

Victorian Quilters
PO Box 264
Essendon North VIC 3041

Tasmanian Quilting Guild
c/o 20 Manor Gardens
Kings Meadows TAS 7249

NEW ZEALAND
National Association of New Zealand Quilters
c/o 32 Tainui Road
Devonport
Auckland

UNITED STATES
American Quilting Society
Box 3290
Paducah
Kentucky 42002-3290

National Quilting Association
PO Box 393
Ellicott City
Maryland 21041-0393

American International Quilt Association
7660 Woodway Drive, Suite 550
Houston
Texas 77063

QUILTING SUPPLIERS AND EQUIPMENT
The companies listed below stock a good range of materials for quilting. Many also supply goods by mail order. Other manufacturers and suppliers of quilting equipment are featured in advertisements found in specialist quilting magazines.

GREAT BRITAIN
Country Threads
2 Pierrepoint Place
Bath BA1 1JX

John Lewis
Oxford Street
London W1A 1EX

Pansy Pins
159 Main Street
Uddington
Glasgow G71 7BP

Quilt Basics
2 Meades Lane
Chesham
Bucks HP5 1ND

The Cotton Patch
1285 Stratford Road
Hall Green
Birmingham B28 9AJ

The Quilt Room
20 West Street
Dorking
Surrey RH4 1BL

Redburn Crafts
Squares Garden Centre
Halliford Road
Upper Halliford
Shepperton
Middlesex TW17 8RU

Village Fabrics
Unit 7 Bushnell Business Estate
Hithercroft
Lester Way
Wallingford
Oxon OX10 9DP

UNITED STATES
American Patchwork and Quilting
Catalog Dept A9603
Box 6656
Maple Plain
Minniapolis 55592-6656

Hancock Fabrics
3841 Hinkleville Road
Paducah
Kentucky 42002-3290

House of White Birches
306 East Pharr Road
Berne
Indiana 46711

Keepsake Quilting
Route 25B
PO Box 1618
Centre Harbor
New Hampshire 03226-1618

MAGAZINES
Specialist quilting magazines are good sources of information about patterns, materials and techniques. They also include addresses of mail order companies and shops specialising in quilting materials.

GREAT BRITAIN
Patchwork & Quilting
Traplet House
Severn Drive
Upton-upon-Severn
Worcestershire WR08 0JL

Popular Patchwork
Nexus Special Interest Ltd
Nexus House
Boundary Way
Hemel Hempstead
HP2 7ST

AUSTRALIA AND NEW ZEALAND
Australian Patchwork and Quilting
2 Stanley Street
Silverwater NSW 2144
Tel: (02) 9748 0599

Down Under Quilts
PO Box 145
Baulkham Hills NSW 2153
Tel: (02) 9838 9806

New Zealand Quilter
PO Box 5246
Lambton Quay

Wellington
New Zealand
Tel: (04) 389 3207

UNITED STATES
American Quilter
Box 3290
Subscriptions
Paducah KY 42002-3290

American Patchwork and Quilting
Subscriptions
1912 Grand Avenue
Des Moins, Iowa 50309-3379

Old Fashioned Patchwork
Harris Publications Inc
1115 Broadway
NY NY 10010

Traditional Quilter
Box 507
Subscriptions
Mt Morris Ill 61054

Quiltmaker
Subscriptions
Box 58360
Boulder Co 80322-8360

Quilting Today
Box 1376
Subscriptions
Riverton NJ 08076-0615

Traditional Quiltworks
PO Box 10615
Subscriptions
Riverton NJ 08076-0615

Quilters Newsletter Magazine
Box 59021
Boulder CO 80322-9021

Ladies Circle Patchwork Quilts
Box 516
Subscriptions
Mt Morris Ill 61045

INDEX

Accuracy test, seams, 17
Analogous colours, 15
Appliqué, 12
   techniques, 25
   templates, 16
Assembling quilts, 26-9
Assembly line piecing, 20
Attached binding finish, 33

Baby Quilt, Nine Patch and Hearts, 60-3
Backing fabric, 8, 13, 28
Backstitch, 32
Bag, Flying Geese, 106-9
Bargello Jewellery Pouch, 80-3
Basting, 29
Batting, 8, 13, 28-9
Bear's Paw, 38, 41, 42
Bias grain, 13
Binding, of edges, 33-5
Birds in the Air, 38, 40, 41
Blindstitch, 25
Blocks, 12
   making a sample block, 16
   names, 12
   setting together in rows, 27
Bonded machine appliqué, 25
Borders, 27
Bunny Quilt, 56-9

Chequerboards, strip pieced, 20
Chevrons, strip pieced, 21
Colours:
   blending, 114
   complementary, 15
   harmonies, 15
   schemes, 14-15
   wheel, 15
Computers, 10
Continuous prairie point borders, 34-5
Corners, mitring, 33
Cotton thread, 11
Country Basket Quilt, 64-7
Country Kitchen accessories, 44-7
Crazy patchwork, 23
Crossgrain, 13
Curved line quilting, 31-2

Cutting mats, 10
Cutting techniques, 18-19

Delectable Mountains Quilt, 14, 52-5
Diamonds, strip pieced, 21
Displaying quilts, 36
Dying, with tea, 113

Edges, binding, 33-5
Equipment, 10-11

Fabrics, 8
   choosing, 13
   cutting from templates, 16
   preparation, 13
   types, 13
   widths, 8, 12
Fast grid triangles, 22
54-40 or Fight, 38, 40, 42
Finishing techniques, 33-6
Five Patch design, 12
Flying Geese Bag, 106-9
Foundations:
   material, 11
   piecing, 23
Four Patch design, 12
Frames, 29
Free-motion quilting, 31
Freezer paper, 11,16, 25
Fusible web, 11

Grain, on fabric, 13
Granny Smith's Log Cabin Quilt, 92-5
Grids:
   for fast grid triangles, 22
   quilted, 31

Half square triangles, 22
Hand-tied quilts, 32
Hanging sleeves, 36
Hoops, 11

Iris Sampler Picnic Cloth, 14, 38-43

Jewellery Pouch, Bargello, 80-3

Kitchen accessories, 44-7

Layering, of the quilt, 29
Lengthwise grain, 13
Log cabin patchwork, 24
Lone Star Wall Hanging, 84-7
Long strips, cutting, 18

Machine, using for:
   appliqué, 25
   patchwork, 20
   quilting, 30-2
Machine-tied quilts, 32
Marking, of the quilt top, 30
Measurements, 8
Mitring:
   of borders, 27
   of corners, 33
Moleskin, 17

Needles, 11
Nine Patch design, 12, 38, 40
Nine Patch and Hearts Baby Quilt, 60-3

Ohio Star design, 38, 41, 42
Ohio Star Quilt, 48-51
One Patch designs, 12
Outline quilting, 31

Painting, on Reindeer Quilt, 88-91
Paper, 11
   foundation piecing, 23
   freezer, 11, 16, 25
   paper-backed fusible web, 11
Patchwork:
   piecing techniques, 20-4
   templates, 16
Patterns, 12
Pieced quilts, 12
   techniques, 20-4
Pineapple Cushion, 96-9
Pins, 11
Points, matching up, 26
Posts, 27
Prairie point borders
(see Continuous prairie point borders)
Prints, scale, 14

Quarter square triangles, 22
Quick reference guide, 8
Quilted grids, 31
Quilting frames, 29
Quilting-in-the-ditch, 31

Rail Fence Wall Hanging, 14, 68-71
Rectangles, cutting, 19
Reindeer Quilt, 88-91
Rolling Star, 38, 41
Rotary cutters, 10, 18
Rotary mats, 10, 18
Rotary rulers, 10, 18
Rows, sewing together, 27

Safety pins, 11
    basting the layers with, 29
Sample blocks, 17
Sashes, 27
Satin stitch, 25
Sawtooth Star, 38, 40
Scale, prints, 14
Seams:
    accuracy test, 17
    matching up, 26

quilting-in-the-ditch, 31
    seam allowances, 16, 17
Self-binding finish, 33
Selvages, 13
Seminole Photo Album Cover, 72-5
Set-in patches, 26
Sewing techniques, 17
Shoo Fly, 38, 41, 42
Skill levels, for projects, 8
Sleeves, hanging, 36
Snowball block, 50
Split complementary colours, 15
Squares, cutting, 19
Star of Bethlehem, 84
Stencilling, Bunny Quilt, 56-9
Stipple quilting, 32
Stitches:
    appliqué, 25
    curved line, 31
    free-motion, 31
    outline, 31
    quilting-in-the-ditch, 31
    stipple, 32
    straight line, 30
    straight stitch, 25

String piecing, 23
Strip piecing, 20-1
Strips, cutting, 18-19
Sunshine and Shadows Quilt, 76-9

Table Runner, Crazy Quilted, 100-1
Tea dying, 113
Techniques, 17-36
Templates, 8, 118-24
    making and using, 16
    positioning, 13
    stencilling, 58
    template plastic, 10
Thimbles, 11
Tied quilts, 32
Tools, 10-11
Triadic colours, 15
Triangles:
    cutting, 19
    fast grid, 22
Turn-and-sew, 24

Walking foot, 30
Wall hangings, 36
Whole cloth quilts, 12